HEPBURN
Her Life in Pictures

JAMES SPADA

DOUBLEDAY & COMPANY, INC.
GARDEN CITY, NEW YORK
1984

Books of related interest by James Spada

Judy and Liza
Monroe: Her Life in Pictures
Streisand: The Woman and the Legend
The Films of Robert Redford
Barbra: The First Decade

Designed by Laurence Alexander

Library of Congress Cataloging in Publication Data
Spada, James.
Hepburn, her life in pictures.

1. Hepburn, Katharine, DATE —Portraits,
caricatures, etc.   I. Title.
PN2287.H45S65   1984   791.43′028′0924 [B]   83-25444
ISBN #0-385-18789-0
ISBN 0-385-18790-4 (A Dolphin book: pbk.)

Acknowledgments

Special gratitude is reserved for Ben Carbonetto and Sandra Quinn, whose extensive and lovingly maintained collections on Katharine Hepburn contributed importantly to this book.

Thanks to Karen Swenson, Chris Nickens, Dan Conlon, J. B. Annegan, Delia Moon, Ken deBie, John Cusimano, Vernon Patterson, Guy Vespoint, Greg Rice, Michel Parenteau, Lou Valentino, George Zeno, Bruce Mandes, John Fricke, Terry Miller, Homer Dickens, Lanny Sher, Jeff Schaffer, Michael Hawks, Paul O'Driscoll, and the staff of the Academy of Motion Pictures Arts and Sciences Library.

Fond appreciation to those who helped see this book along its way: Kathy Robbins, Laura Van Wormer, Larry Alexander, Doug Bergstreser, Michael Lupow, Loretta Fidel, Richard Covey, Jack Dwosh, Marilyn Ducksworth, Deb Alter.

I wish to extend my appreciation to Mary Flint and Actors and Others for Animals for their permission to reproduce Katharine Hepburn's self-portrait "Lizzie." Actors and Others for Animals is a worthy charity which has the full support of Ms. Hepburn. Anyone desiring to make a contribution may write to them at: 12444 Ventura Blvd., Studio City, CA 91604.

Dedicated with love to my grandmother, Carmela Ruberto Trapanese who turned 100 this year.

Contents

HEPBURN

———————

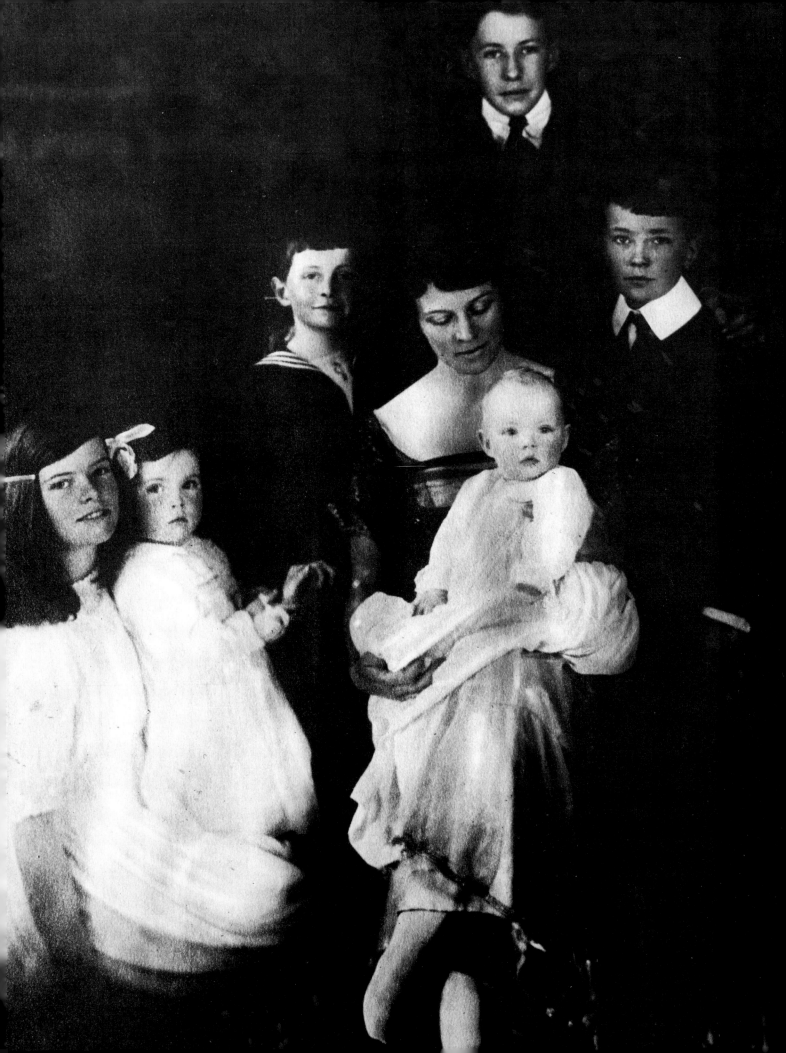

Part One

MAVERICK

1907–1932

They were, by any standards, a maverick clan. The Hepburns of Hartford continually scandalized their strait-laced society counterparts with their liberal attitudes and Mrs. Hepburn's passionate campaigning for women's suffrage. "My mother was considered a dangerous and wicked woman," Katharine Hepburn later recalled. "When I was a small child, we'd meet a neighbor on the street. My mother would say 'Good Morning,' and the neighbor would look through us as if nobody was there. My mother didn't mind."

Dr. Thomas Hepburn and the former Katharine Houghton were married in 1904, and within a year had a son, Thomas. Three years later, on November 8, 1907, Katharine Houghton Hepburn was born. The family was rounded out during the next five years with two more boys, Robert and Richard, and two girls, Peggy and Marion.

"I was brought up great," Katharine says, "just great. I had a *fascinating* mother, a *fascinating* father, and a wonderful childhood."

Dr. Hepburn was a man who considered ignorance one of the greatest threats to the health and welfare of the world. He campaigned to enlighten the public about birth control and prevention of venereal disease, two more topics one was not supposed to discuss in "polite company." Not only did he discuss these issues with his peers, but with his children as well. No topic was forbidden in the Hepburn household, and all his children were encouraged to ask questions and add their opinions to the discourse—"but not idiotically," Kate adds.

It was little wonder that young "Kathy" quickly developed into a very unusual little girl. She was headstrong, athletic, not only a tomboy but something of a roughneck. She wore her brother's clothes and once shaved her head because her bangs put her at a disadvantage when she wrestled.

For all their liberal social attitudes, the Hepburns had a strong Spartan streak. Dr. Hepburn believed in physical strength and fitness, and held disdain for many creature comforts. His children were not coddled; if

---

OPPOSITE Kate at age two with Tom in the Connecticut woods.

OPPOSITE PART ONE Mrs. Hepburn poses with her children shortly before Tom's death. Left to right are Kate, Marion, Robert, Tom, Richard, and baby Peggy.

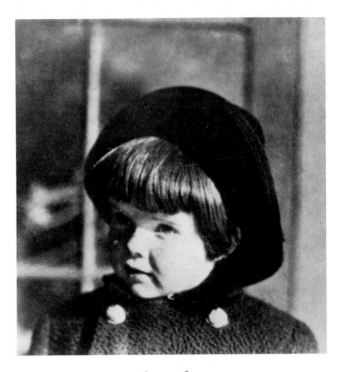

At age four.

---

they complained of illness, they were told to lie down until they felt better. Every morning began with an icy shower. It is clear that the famous Katharine Hepburn traits—common sense, clear-headedness, athletic ability, liberalism—were a Hepburn child's birthright.

But other Hepburn trademarks—stoicism, an incredible ability to convey suffering, that empathy with sadness—came later, when Kate was just twelve. She idolized her brother Tom, a handsome, athletic, intelligent boy whom Kate felt closer to than anyone else. During the Easter Season of 1920, Tom and Kate vacationed in New York and saw *A Connecticut Yankee in King Arthur's Court*. Fifteen-year-old Tom was very much impressed by the hero's ability to survive a hanging by flexing his neck muscles so that the rope wouldn't cut off his air supply.

Easter day, back in Hartford, Kate went looking for her brother when he didn't show up at the breakfast table. She found him in the attic, hanging from a rope tied to a rafter. He was dead. No one could imagine any reason Tom Hepburn would have had to kill himself, and the official explanation was that he had made a foolish attempt to emulate the feat he had seen during that New York play.

Suddenly, Kate Hepburn was no longer a carefree girl. She became despondent and listless, her grades fell off, her family worried about her. It wasn't until that summer, when she discovered the world of make-believe, that she came out of her depression. Young Katharine Hepburn started to perform in local children's theater, and the actress began to emerge.

Eleven-year-old Katharine in 1918.

By the time Kate was eighteen, the celebrated Hepburn cheekbones had begun to develop, and so had her strong talent in athletics. She had already won a bronze medal for figure skating and competed in the semifinals of the Connecticut Young Women's Golf Championship. Although she had been putting on shows—acting, writing, producing, and collecting the box-office receipts—her professed ambition at this point in her life was to be a doctor.

Hepburn as Pandora in the Bryn Mawr production of the Elizabethan pastoral *Woman in the Moone*. She entered the exclusive women's college, her mother's Alma Mater, in 1924, at seventeen. She fared rather poorly as an academic—"I had an airy mind"—but when she learned that a B average was required for participation in extracurricular activities, her grades improved.

The activity she wanted to participate in, of course, was dramatics. Her first two efforts were not as memorable as her third. She played Pandora and was warmly received by her audience. In flowing gown, a wreath of laurels crowning her red hair, she bore the pain of gravel under her feet like a trouper, refusing her director's suggestion that she wear sandals. "Pandora went barefoot," she retorted. "And so shall I."

By now, she had decided that she would be an actress. It was a decision she knew would appall her father; all show business, in the Hepburn household, was considered little better than the traveling sideshow variety, and was certainly unworthy of a young woman of Katharine Hepburn's station. She waited to tell her parents of her decision until after her performance in *Woman in the Moone,* as she was driving with them back to Connecticut. They had enjoyed the show, but their daughter's pronouncement came as a total surprise.

Mrs. Hepburn—much as Katharine suspected—was secretly pleased by her daughter's rebellious attitude, but Dr. Hepburn was, indeed, horrified. Father and daughter argued for miles, and Kate finally burst into bitter tears. "All right!" he bellowed. "I'll give you fifty dollars to get started, but that's all!"

ABOVE Shortly after her graduation from Bryn Mawr in the spring of 1928, Hepburn began her professional career in Edwin Knopf's summer stock company in Baltimore. She appeared briefly in two plays, one without any lines, the other with just a few. But those few proved problematic for her. Her nervousness often caused her voice to rise several octaves without reason or warning; a sympathetic stage manager advised her to seek voice lessons in New York. She did.

Hepburn's Broadway debut was supposed to be as the star of *The Big Pond,* a Knopf production. (She is shown here with Marie Curtis in a rehearsal shot.) Despite Katharine's woeful lack of experience, Knopf felt her striking looks and presence would carry the day, and they almost did. Things went swimmingly on the first night of out-of-town tryouts, until a well-delivered Hepburn line got the first big laugh of the evening. She was thrown by it and was never able to re-

(continued on page 8)

cover; she began to recite her lines so rapidly no one could understand her. She was fired that night.

Hepburn's next vehicle, *These Days,* did make it to Broadway, and she survived opening night (November 12, 1928) without mishap. But the show closed in just eight days. "I didn't realize then that shows folded up," Hepburn has said. "I thought they sort of opened and then went on indefinitely."

On December 12, 1928, Kate impetuously married Ludlow Ogden Smith, a Philadelphian Main Liner who agreed to change his name to Ogden Ludlow so that his wife would not be referred to as "Kate Smith."

Hepburn decided to give up her career, and gave notice to the producer of *Holiday* (a show for which she understudied), but within two months she was dreadfully bored and asked to be rehired. For all intents and purposes, her marriage at this point was over, but she and "Luddy" did not divorce until 1934, and remained friends all his life.

Never was Hepburn's subsequent quest for privacy more successful than in keeping her husband out of the public eye. No public pictures have ever been taken of them together.

PREVIOUS PAGES Hepburn in the 1930 Broadway production *Art and Mrs. Bottle,* with veteran actress Jane Cowl and G. P. Huntley, Jr. Few of the people Kate encountered in this new milieu knew what to make of her. She seemed at first aristocratic and snobby, and she made things worse by affecting an air of hauteur in order to hide her nervousness. Most of her directors took an instant dislike to her. Benn Levy, author of this play, fired her in short order: "She looks a fright, her manner is objectionable, and she has no talent." But after testing fourteen other actresses, he rehired Kate; none of those other women had her *presence—* love her or loathe her, one certainly noticed her.

Hepburn's critical reception in *Art and Mrs. Bottle* seemed designed to counter Levy's objections almost directly. Howard Barnes of the New York *Herald Tribune* called her "agreeable to look at, assured, and altogether a proficient actress."

OPPOSITE Hepburn as Antiope in the 1932 sex-role reversal comedy *The Warrior's Husband,* wherein a group of very aggressive fighting Amazons keep their husbands in place. It was a perfect role for Hepburn, requiring athletic prowess, masculine demeanor, and a stronger stage presence than her male co-stars—just the things that had turned many people against her in her previous stage appearances.

She made a memorable entrance, running down a ramp and throwing a dead deer off her shoulder onto the floor in front of her tribe leader. Other feats of physical agility and strength—including lifting one of the actors over her head—left the audience cheering Kate at show's end. Robert Garland, in the New York *World-Telegram,* raved, "Miss Katharine Hepburn comes into her own as Antiope. Ever since she supported Miss Jane Cowl in *Art and Mrs. Bottle,* I've been waiting for (her) to fall heir to a role worthy of her talent and beauty. Antiope is that role . . . It's been many a night since so glowing a performance brightened the Broadway scene."

FOLLOWING PAGES With Colin Keith-Johnston, *The Warrior's Husband* ran for eighty-three performances, long enough for Kate to be seen by many influential show business people. Quickly, Hollywood's budding film industry took notice. Twentieth Century-Fox bought the rights to the play, and Hepburn did a screen test for them. She lost the role to Elissa Landi, which was just as well with her: Hepburn, like most theater people of the day, looked upon Hollywood with disdain. She turned down a well-paying contract from Paramount Studios, intending to remain on the stage.

RKO Pictures, however, asked her to test for a movie role opposite John Barrymore, and she was intrigued. The test was greeted with derision by most studio executives—they thought Hepburn looked "like a cross between a horse and a monkey"—and Kate later admitted the test was badly done: "There was something awfully heartbreaking about the girl I was in those days. I was trying hard—too hard. I was so eager—too eager."

But, as fate would have it, George Cukor, set to direct the film, was moved by a small gesture of Hepburn's and urged that she be hired. Not sure about making the move, and to test how badly she was wanted, Hepburn demanded the outrageous sum of fifteen hundred dollars a week to make the picture. (She was making $75 a week in *The Warrior's Husband.*)

The studio's first counteroffer was seven hundred and fifty dollars, but Kate held firm until they met her demand. "They must be insane out there!" Kate exclaimed to her best friend, Laura Harding, upon hearing the news. She prevailed upon Laura to accompany her, and the two left for California by train.

It was a career decision that would change Katharine Hepburn's life forever.

Part Two

RELUCTANT
CELEBRITY

1932–1936

Katharine Hepburn arrives in Pasadena, California, July 1932. She had hoped to make a grand impression on her new agent, Leland Hayward, and Myron Selznick (brother of David Selznick, the head of RKO), who came to meet her, but this was not to be. The trip was a tiring one, and Kate had gotten a cinder in her eye on the train's observation platform. She arrived quite weary, with both eyes inflamed. Her outfit—which she thought was the height of chic—did little to flatter her.

As Hepburn climbed into the chauffeured limousine that was to take her to the studio, Selznick muttered, "My God. Are we sticking David fifteen hundred dollars a week for *that?*"

Stung by the insult, Hepburn turned defensively imperious, even with George Cukor, who met her at the studio and was one of her only allies. Infuriated by her arrogant rejection of clothes designed for her, Cukor told her that in the "ghastly" ensemble she was wearing, she shouldn't be so quick to criticize.

"The first thing I'm going to do," he told the startled Kate, "is to get you into makeup, so they can do something about your hair!"

Hepburn, Hollywood style. They did something about her hair, her makeup, her eyes. As the hairdresser was undoing her topknot, Kate said, "There's nothing you can do about it. It's baby hair." The stylist told her it was beautiful hair, and proceeded to bob it. Kate loved the results. Cukor, sticking his head in every so often to watch the transformation, got some unexpected advice from the makeup man, who was extremely taken with Hepburn: "She has natural looks, high cheekbones, and whatever you do, don't put a voice coach on her. Her diction is absolutely unique. Audiences will love it."

When the job was done, everyone was pleased. "Well," Cukor beamed, "there's Katharine Hepburn at last."

Hepburn and Barrymore in *A Bill of Divorcement*. There were bound to be great stories arising out of this meeting of a staunchly individualistic Yankee and a legendarily egotistical talent, and so there are. Upon meeting Hepburn her first day on the studio lot, Barrymore noticed her red eyes and took her aside conspiratorially. He told her that when he drank, he used eye drops to hide the telltale redness in his eyes.

"But, Mr. Barrymore," Kate protested, "I have a cinder in my eye."

"Yes, dear," Barrymore replied. "That's what they all say."

Another time Barrymore, an infamous womanizer, is reputed to have invited Hepburn to his dressing room and then exposed himself to her. When she expressed her shock, dismay, and lack of interest ("My father doesn't want me to make babies!") Barrymore, ego bruised, told her "any young girl would be thrilled to make love to the great John Barrymore." Hepburn remained unimpressed.

Once, on the set, Barrymore pinched Kate's behind. She protested, "If you do that again, I'm going to stop acting."

Barrymore replied, "I wasn't aware that you'd started, my dear."

Despite these and other reports of conflict between the two stars, Hepburn has said that Barrymore was a

Billie Burke and Kate in a scene from *A Bill of Divorcement*. The story concerns a man (Barrymore) whose war experiences bring out his latent insanity. He escapes from an asylum and returns home on the day his ex-wife (Burke) is to marry another man. He realizes he cannot win back his wife, but his daughter (Hepburn) vows to stay with him and care for him, breaking her engagement for fear that her children might be afflicted by her father's hereditary mental illness.

Director Cukor was quite impressed with his young star. "Kate had absolutely no film experience, but she seemed immediately at home in front of the camera. [In a scene] Barrymore was playing her shell-shocked father—a virtual stranger to her since she was a child. She looked at him with the most enormous tenderness, and her eyes filled with tears. After that scene, Jack and I gave each other a look of 'O.K.' We knew we had latched on to something very special."

tremendous help to her. "(He) never criticized me. He just shoved me into what I ought to do. He taught me all that he could pour into one greenhorn in that short a time."

15

Another glamour look at Hepburn, 1932. From the beginning, Kate refused to go along with the "Hollywood game"—publicity stunts, charming interviews, parties, premieres. She was quickly nicknamed "Katharine of Arrogance" by many in the community, who saw her attitude as snobbery.

October 17, 1932, Hepburn returns from a three-week tour of Europe with Luddy Smith. RKO had wired her frantically to come back, in order to capitalize on the swirl of favorable attention being paid to her performance in *A Bill of Divorcement*. Kate indeed cut her trip short, but RKO may have regretted it. Upset by the probing personal questions of reporters, Hepburn gave flip responses. Asked if she and Luddy were married, she replied, "I don't remember." Asked if she had any children, she answered, "Yes—two white and three colored." As is so often the case, her attitude, born of discomfort with publicity and a desire to avoid newsmen, just made her that much more pressworthy. From this point on, she would be hounded continually by reporters and cameramen.

PREVIOUS PAGES With David Manners as her fiancé. *A Bill of Divorcement* was a major hit, and so was Hepburn. Her odd manner and voice, and her stunning beauty—brought out breathtakingly by cinematographer Sid Hickox—startled audiences and critics alike. Richard Watts in the New York *Herald Tribune* wrote, "Mr. Barrymore, showing surprising restraint when you remember that he is a Barrymore playing a madman, is splendid as the escaped father . . . The most effective portrayal of the film, however, is provided by Miss Katharine Hepburn, who is both beautiful and distinguished as the daughter, and seems definitely established for an important cinema career."

OPPOSITE On the RKO lot, Hepburn poses in an outfit that rather neatly sums up the warring elements of her personality: the jeans, her usual mode of dress, were her way of showing Hollywood that she wasn't about to give in totally to its glamorous demands. But, then again, she wasn't above interest in a plush fur coat— or the Hispano-Suiza touring car she rented to transport her and Laura Harding to the set each day. She was embarrassed to learn that it was a prop car which had become something of an inside joke and didn't impress the community at all. But typically for Hepburn, she refused to replace it and continued to ride grandly around in its huge back seat.

A rare shot of Hepburn as "bathing beauty." The photograph was taken as publicity for what was supposed to be her next film, *Three Came Unarmed,* with Joel McCrea. RKO decided that in view of the excitement her first screen appearance had generated, she deserved a full starring role, and they cast her instead in the film version of the Gilbert Frankau novel *Christopher Strong*.

As aviatrix Lady Cynthia Darrington in *Christopher Strong*. The film's melodramatic plot revolves around Lady Cynthia and her love for a married man. Upon learning she is pregnant by him, and unwilling to break up his marriage, she takes off in her plane and removes her oxygen mask, performing the ultimate act of selfless love.

Despite the film's questionable plot, Lady Cynthia presented a perfect role for Hepburn—a strong, career-oriented, independent woman.

FOLLOWING PAGES Dressed as an insect for a costume-party scene in the film. Making *Christopher Strong* was not a pleasant experience for Kate. She didn't get along with director Dorothy Arzner, who—as one of the few women directors in Hollywood—performed her task with a grim determination that turned her set into a vat of tensions; and, despite Arzner's professed desire to "soften" Hepburn's screen image, she comes off brittle and uncomfortable in the film.

Some reviewers commented on this. William Boehnel of the New York *World-Telegram* said he was "aghast at the amateur quality of her histrionics. For the first half of the film, she shrieks her lines in an unduly affected voice, for the rest of the time, her diction. . . jars the nerves."

OPPOSITE The striking Hepburn beauty, 1932.

(continued on page 24)

With her gibbon, Amos, on the RKO lot. Animal lovers Kate and Laura Harding shared a Hollywood house which was something of a menagerie.

Hepburn and Douglas Fairbanks, Jr., perform *Romeo and Juliet* in a play-within-the-movie scene from *Morning Glory*. Fairbanks acted a young playwright with whom Hepburn falls in love after breaking off an affair with producer Adolphe Menjou. According to Fairbanks, he disliked Hepburn at first, resenting all the attention this newcomer was getting. But soon, he says, he fell "head over heels" in love with her. She refused his first few requests for a date, then gave in, only to develop a "headache" on their night out. Fairbanks drove her home but, as he told Hepburn biographer Charles Higham, he didn't leave right away. "I wanted to savor the experience of having dated Katharine Hepburn, thinking about her, feeling her close, seeing her, hearing her." Fairbanks expected to see the lights go out, but instead Kate came running out and jumped into a car Fairbanks hadn't seen farther up the driveway. "I saw a man at the wheel," Fairbanks said. "I never saw his face. They drove right past me without even noticing me. She was laughing happily, her hair blowing over her face. That was why she had cut her date short!"

(continued from page 21)

There were good reviews for Hepburn, more so than for the film: Regina Crew, in the New York *American,* commented: "That troubled, masque-like face, the high, strident, raucous, rasping voice, the straight, broad-shouldered boyish figure—perhaps they all may grate upon you, but they compel attention, and they fascinate an audience. She is a distinct, definite, positive personality—the first since Garbo."

Christopher Strong was not a big hit at the box office—as with so many Hepburn heroines of the thirties, America wasn't ready to warm up to Lady Cynthia—but her screen charisma was once again amply demonstrated.

Adolphe Menjou and Kate in a publicity pose for *Morning Glory*. Hepburn's third film represented a perfect melding of actress and role: she played Eva Lovelace, a struggling young actress enamored of the theater who encounters rejection after rejection but perseveres. Watching the film now, one senses that Katharine Hepburn was playing herself of just a few years earlier. "There will always be a Shaw play in my repertoire as long as I remain in the theater," Eva says. "And of course, I shall die in the theater. My star will never set."

FOLLOWING PAGES Kate rehearses the scene in which a tipsy Eva Lovelace performs the balcony scene from *Romeo and Juliet* at a party in order to demonstrate her enormous talent.

Morning Glory gave Hepburn a marvelous acting opportunity; she is frightened and meek at the outset, starry-eyed and willing to sacrifice for her art as her struggles mount, grandly theatrical after a few drinks at the party, and touchingly resigned as she is forced to choose between the career she has so longed for and the love of a man.

Although there was criticism of the "depressing limitations of a second-rate story," reviewers were lavish in their praise for Hepburn. *Time* summed up the general reaction well: "From this immemorial fairy tale, the delicate, muscled face of Heroine Hepburn stands out like a face on a coin. Of the brash little provincial she makes a strangely distinguished character, a little mad from hunger and dreams, absurdly audacious and trusting. Since *Christopher Strong,* she has toned down her strident voice, taken off some of her angular swank in gesture and strut, found other ways to register emotion than dilating her nostrils."

The superbly dramatic Hepburn, captured by a studio photographer in 1933. Hollywood, which hadn't known what to make of Kate Hepburn at first, officially welcomed her into its hallowed inner circle by awarding her the 1933 Best Actress Oscar. She was only the sixth actress so honored, and it would be thirty-four years later before she would win her second.

Hepburn did not attend the award ceremonies. "I had sent them a wire through my agent Leland Hayward, to say that I didn't believe in awards, and that I didn't really feel that I should compete—some pompous, asinine thing. He just put the wire in his pocket and said, 'Thank you very much,' that I was deeply honored. He changed the wire because he thought it was childish. I often wonder whether we behave so ungraciously because we really think that we should have been given a prize for every performance."

Another date with Douglas Fairbanks, Jr., this one for publicity purposes. The occasion was a private film screening at Jesse Lasky's beach house, late 1933.

OPPOSITE "Kate Hepburn was born to play the part": George Cukor on Jo March of *Little Women*. If Eva Lovelace represented the aspiring actress in Kate, Louisa May Alcott's enduringly popular tomboy heroine was the absolute personification of Hartford's most rambunctious daughter. "Kate cast a spell of magic and a kind of power over the picture," Cukor says. "You could go with whatever she did. She really felt it all very deeply. She's a New England girl who understands all that and has her own family feeling."

The March girls: Joan Bennett as Amy, Kate as Jo, Jean Parker as Beth, and Frances Dee as Meg (with Mabel Colcord as Hannah, the maid). All the young women in the film were newcomers, but Kate, like Jo, became their inspiration. Frances Dee recalls, "Sometimes while she was reading or just contemplating alone, we girls . . . would creep up and peek at her, absolutely awestruck by her concentration. I'm sure she knew we were watching, but she never looked up or around."

On this film, Hepburn began a practice which she would continue for years: bringing picnic lunches every day for all the cast and crew. It must have been expensive, and time-consuming work for Laura Harding and their maid Joanna, but it made for a pleasant lunch break and endeared Kate to everyone.

The caption accompanying this studio publicity photograph reads: "Katharine Hepburn marches to awe-inspiring dramatic heights in the most exacting role known to American literature—that of Jo in Louisa May Alcott's eternal bestseller, *Little Women,* the newest Hepburn-vivified picturization achieved by RKO Radio Studios."

Whew. Despite all that, Hepburn's performance *was* marvelous, a perfect blending of girlish high spirits, staunch independence and responsibility, sensitivity to the suffering of others and a strength of character still rare for women on the screen. The movie proved to be Hepburn's first unqualified box-office smash, and it further elevated her rising stock in Hollywood.

OPPOSITE In a scene from the Broadway production *The Lake,* December 1933. Ever since she became a star in Hollywood, Hepburn had longed to return to the stage. *The Lake,* the story of a young woman who rediscovers family loyalty after an accident, seemed like the perfect vehicle for her, and she was anxious to work with director Jed Harris.

The production, however, proved to be one of Kate's most disastrous professional experiences. She and Harris had very little artistic compatibility; he found her maddeningly artificial and concerned only with externals, a condition he blamed entirely on Hollywood. Impartial observers, however, say he "brutalized"

Hepburn, shaking her confidence in her performance to the point that externals were the only thing she could rely on. One witness to the rehearsals said, "If she turned her head to the left, he didn't like it. If she turned it to the right, he liked it still less."

By the time *The Lake* opened in New York on the day after Christmas, 1933, Kate was emotionally exhausted. She began the play in a state of near hysteria, so that climactic dramatic scenes were played with the same level of emotion as the initial scenes. It was about this play that Dorothy Parker made her now-famous observation of Hepburn: "She ran the gamut of emotions from A to B."

(continued on page 32)

A sultry Hepburn, early 1934.

Kate and Leland Hayward in a January 1934 candid. For years, this heavily retouched photo has been incorrectly identified as one of Hepburn and her husband, Ludlow Ogden Smith. By this time, however, she was involved in a serious romance with Hayward. Hepburn kept dates as secret as possible, insisting that her private life was none of anyone else's business.

Hayward was one of Hollywood's most successful agents, a dashing, sophisticated, intelligent man with whom Kate was quite smitten. He was never faithful to her, seeing a bevy of other women, including actress Margaret Sullavan, whom he later married. But many observers have said that next to Spencer Tracy, Leland Hayward was the most important romance in Katharine Hepburn's life.

(continued from page 30)

Near the end of the play's run of fifty-five performances, Kate's acting improved—with the help of her drama coach Frances Robinson-Duff—but it was too late: the play closed. Kate felt she was well rid of it, and was astonished by a rumor that despite the show's lukewarm reception (the production itself was criticized as much as Kate), Harris intended to take it on the road. When Hepburn called him to ask if this were true, he said yes, and added, "My dear, the only interest I have in you is the money I can make out of you."

Kate asked him how much he would take to let her out of her contract. "How much have you got?" he asked in reply. Kate put down the phone, looked in her checkbook, and said, "I've got exactly fifteen thousand, four hundred and sixty-one dollars and sixty-seven cents."

Harris took a check for that exact amount and Kate never saw or heard from him again.

OPPOSITE As Trigger Hicks in *Spitfire*. Hepburn's fifth film represented a complete departure for her: she played a simple, uneducated mountain girl who believes she has mystical healing powers. Although Kate's reviews were good, the role was really too much of a stretch. Even the film's director, John Cromwell, has since said, "The picture has absolutely nothing to recommend it. The part of Trigger Hicks is about as unsuited to Katharine's talents as anything that can be imagined."

A publicity portrait for *Spitfire*. Hepburn's acting in the film was generally praised, although her New England accent too often broke through her attempts at Ozark dialect. The film was an unqualified box-office disaster, the first of many such disappointments for Kate in the thirties. The *Times* of London offered a perceptive analysis of her personality, still quite new to audiences: "In the wide world of the cinema, the art of Miss Katharine Hepburn has too small a place—small, perhaps, because she has never courted popularity by appearing in a quick succession of sophisticated and sentimental stories. Popularity means little to her; she is content with films that do not require her to throw away her rare gift of being able to touch in us an emotion usually free from the sentimentality which audiences have become accustomed to expect. She creates a feeling in her audience by a kind of vital expectation which causes a feeling to flow towards her."

By now, Katharine Hepburn was a woman of tremendous interest to the American people. Whenever she appeared in public, newspapermen were always present, to take her picture and ask her questions. Later, she would go to great lengths to avoid them, but at this juncture in her career her evasive actions were only halfhearted, and she often acted quite graciously toward the press.

Returning from a brief visit to France aboard the SS *Paris* on April 4, 1934, Kate told the press she was thrilled to have won the Oscar, that her favorite actress was Greta Garbo, and that she would soon star in the film *Joan of Arc*. Asked why she had spent just four days in France when she had planned to remain four or five weeks, Kate replied, "I often make these hasty trips. I can't explain why I do it. I just do it and that's all there is to it." Actually, Kate was mortified by the excessive drinking of her traveling companion, former opera singer Suzanne Steele, and couldn't wait to get home.

OPPOSITE Filming a scene with director Cromwell and co-star Robert Young. Hepburn accepted *Spitfire* on the condition that it take no more than four weeks to complete; even one additional day would have cut into her rehearsal time for *The Lake*. When it was clear that the film would go over schedule by a few hours, RKO insisted that those hours still fell within the last day of shooting (it was after five in the afternoon, the usual end of a filming day, but before twelve midnight), and Kate agreed to work until midnight. When the filming still was not completed, however, she refused to work an extra day.

When the studio asked her what she would require to work the extra day, she replied, "Ten thousand dollars." They paid her, and she gave a thousand dollars of it to the Community Fund. "I didn't care so much about the money," she said. "I wanted to show them that when we set a definite date, I meant to keep it, even if they didn't." At the meeting in which she asked for the money, Kate told the studio heads, "You make other people live up to the conditions you write into contracts. It's time you learned to do so, too."

Shortly after her return from New York, Kate and Laura Harding took a quick trip to Mexico, where Kate here takes a photographic back seat to the historic ruins at Uxmal. Kate went to Mexico to obtain a divorce from Ludlow Smith. They both requested that the restriction against remarrying within thirty days be lifted, and the request was granted. The press seized upon the information as proof that Hepburn planned to marry Leland Hayward immediately, but in fact it was Smith who married again within a few days of the divorce.

When she returned to New York on May 3, 1934, Kate was besieged by reporters. At Penn Station she reportedly thumbed her nose at reporters and refused to answer questions. Years later, she told Barbara Walters, in a rare discussion of her short-lived marriage: "I was self-interested. He was a nice man. I felt sorry for him. I say, I broke his heart, spent his money—and my sister took his blood, when she was ill and he was the right type. But we have remained friends all our lives."

The next day, outside her Manhattan townhouse, she was only slightly more loquacious. Reporter: "Are you married?" Hepburn: "Maybe." Reporter: "When you were in Mexico, did you divorce Ludlow Smith?" Hepburn: "Maybe." The wire service caption for this picture was headlined, "It's not the month of May, it's the month of Maybe."

On May 12, Hepburn returned to Los Angeles to begin work on her next film, *The Little Minister*. (Plans to make *Joan of Arc* were abandoned.) "As a conversationalist, Katharine Hepburn rates high," a reporter wrote. "She chatted gaily with everybody, bubbled over with cheerful, humorous incidents of the air voyage, talked readily enough of picture plans—but on the twin subjects of divorce and marriage the steady flow of words came to an end."

OPPOSITE A Hepburn portrait of the period.

On the set with Laura Harding, assistant director Ed Killy, scriptwriter Mort Offner and director Richard Wallace.

Laura Harding had been Kate's best friend since they met in 1928. Kate warmed quickly to Laura's kindness, humor, and athletic high spirits. They were rarely apart, and lived together from the first day Kate arrived in Hollywood. Laura became a fixture on every Hepburn movie set; she usually prepared and served the homemade lunches which had become a staple of Hepburn movie breaks.

After the completion of Kate's next film, however, Laura returned to New York to stay. As much as she adored Kate, Laura Harding was never enamored of the film industry, and she feared she was simply becoming a Hepburn sycophant. "I never even approved of Kate's bohemian ways," Laura later said. But the two remained lifelong friends, seeing each other whenever Kate was on the east coast. Film editor Jane Loring quickly filled the need in Hepburn's life for a female confidante.

OPPOSITE Kate as Lady Babbie in *The Little Minister,* the film in which she may have looked her prettiest and most feminine. She wasn't all that interested at first in playing the James M. Barrie heroine, but when she learned that Margaret Sullavan—her main rival for the affections of Leland Hayward—was also being considered for the role, she went after it. Years later, Kate confided to Dick Cavett: "It became the most important thing in the world to me that I should get it. Several parts in those days I fought for just to take them from someone who needed them."

FOLLOWING PAGES *The Little Minister* revolves around Lady Babbie, an aristocrat in nineteenth-century Scotland who enjoys dressing as a gypsy and mingling with the townsfolk. She sides with the town weavers in a rebellion against her tyrannical stepfather, for whom they work. She meets the new minister of the town, and they find themselves falling in love. The church elders are about to expel the minister when Lady Babbie's true background is revealed.

OPPOSITE John Beal, as the little minister, with Hepburn. The handsome Beal was so taken with Kate that he recalls being unable to summon up anger for a scene in which he was supposed to chastise her. In their first love scene, he underplayed in order not to distract from her. Hepburn pulled him aside afterward and told him, "Don't be afraid to do things on your own. Keep the screen alive."

Beal recalls, "It was a wonderful phrase. She made me feel I needn't be too careful about suppressing my personality. Her electric enthusiasm constantly recharged me."

The Little Minister opened at New York's Radio City Music Hall on December 27, 1934. Andre Sennwald in the New York *Times* summarized the general reaction to the film and gave a clue as to its ultimate box-office failure: "Although dear Babbie's elfin whimsies are likely to cause minor teeth-gnashing among unsympathetic moderns, Miss Hepburn plays the part with likable sprightliness and charm."

Filming *Break of Hearts* with assistant director Jane Loring, director Phillip Moeller and co-star Charles Boyer.

FOLLOWING PAGES As Constance Dane in *Break of Hearts*. The sentimental story concerned a young composer (Hepburn) who marries an eminent conductor (Boyer), leaves him when he's unfaithful, then returns to help him out of alcoholism.

With Charles Boyer in an idyllic honeymoon montage sequence. Hepburn and Boyer got along well; she and her original co-star, Francis Lederer, did not. She could not work with him, finding him slow, but he was kept on the picture until, after two weeks of rehearsal, he refused to come through a doorway because he would show the wrong side of his face. The producers replaced him.

The rather silly *Break of Hearts* was a major box-office flop and *Time* magazine warned, ". . . unless her employers see fit to restore her to roles in keeping with her mannerisms, these will presently annoy cinemaddicts into forgetting that she is really an actress of great promise and considerable style."

Hepburn's career was in some trouble. In a business in which "you're only as good as your last picture," Kate had suffered three ignominious financial failures in a row. Since her last big hit had been *Little Women,* a costume picture, RKO decided that period films were her forte and put her into a series of such pictures, beginning with *Alice Adams.*

As Alice Adams, the Booth Tarkington heroine who aspires to better than she has, Hepburn created one of the most touching characterizations of her career. She was helped along considerably by the direction of George Stevens, heading up his first major production.

The choice of a director had narrowed to Stevens or William Wyler. Pandro Berman, the producer, had a preference for Wyler, but was wary of his reputation for being difficult. Berman had produced five of Kate's first seven films, and they had become quite close. He thinks Kate found Stevens attractive, and so favored him.

When the choice came down to William Wyler or Stevens, Kate agreed to a coin flip. The toss favored Wyler, and she said to Berman: "Let's flip it again." The second time, the choice was Stevens. "Inside us, we both wanted him," Berman says.

With co-star Fred MacMurray in a scene from *Alice Adams*. The story was a simple, touching one: Alice is the sweet, intelligent, refined daughter of a man who is still a clerk after twenty years. She longs for a better life, and fantasizes social importance. She doesn't fit into any stratum of her town's society: her friends find her snobby, her rich acquaintances think of her as beneath them.

After meeting a rich young man (MacMurray), she invites him to dinner, and she and her family go to great pains and expense to impress their guest. Everything that can go wrong does, and Alice is humiliated by the clear fact that she is not what she pretends to be. Despite the fiasco, her suitor refuses to accept that Alice isn't "good enough" for him. Alice sees that he is still interested in her and marvels, "Gee whiz!"

During a break in filming, Hepburn checks her lipstick.

FOLLOWING PAGES A moving moment in *Alice Adams:* after she is ignored at a posh party, she runs upstairs and weeps as rain falls against her bedroom window. It was a scene that caused considerable tension between director and star. Whatever rapport they began with soon evaporated in a clash of styles, and they referred to each other as "Miss Hepburn" and "Mr. Stevens" throughout filming.

In this scene, Kate wanted to throw herself onto her bed and weep into her pillow, her face hidden. Stevens thought it would be more effective if the audience saw Alice cry, and he wanted to juxtapose her tears with the rain outside. Hepburn, uncomfortable with overt displays of emotion, told Stevens that in the same situation, she would fall on her bed. Stevens countered that she wasn't playing herself, but a character whom he felt *would* cry at her window. A shouting match ensued. "It's ridiculous," Kate cried. "There's a limit to stupidity! I've put up with all of it that I can. You dumb son of a bitch, I'm going to cry on the bed!"

Stevens, who previously had directed slapstick, yelled back, "Either you'll cry at the window or I'll return to my custard pies."

"A quitter!" Kate bellowed. "If I ever had any respect for you, it's gone now. You don't get your way so you quit! You're yellow!"

(continued on page 50)

The photos that cost Hepburn a thousand dollars. Flying on November 8, 1935, from L.A. to New York, Kate bet Leland Hayward that amount that she could make the trip without being photographed. All was going well until her plane was forced to make an unscheduled stop in Pittsburgh.

In what must have seemed like a scene from a screwball comedy, Kate spent the layover time in the ladies' room, as a guard stood watch. To avoid photographers again, she clambered out of the bathroom window, aided by a Mr. Peach, pictured here. Unaware that she had been photographed reboarding the plane, Hepburn nearly ran into the propeller trying to elude a photographer after touchdown in New York.

The gleeful caption accompanying these rather bizarre photographs gloated, "By the publication of this picture, she loses the wager."

(continued from page 47)

Stevens would not give in. He had been advised by one of her previous directors: "If you disagree with her, tell her 'No' at least seven times. If you tell her that she might be right, you've lost." He told her to walk to the window and just stand there. He'd film someone else, from behind, and dub the sobbing onto the sound track.

Of course, the moment the cameras began to roll, Kate shed a prodigious quantity of tears.

All the tensions and arguments were well worth it. *Alice Adams,* which opened in August of 1935, was a huge commercial and critical success, and garnered Oscar nominations for Best Picture and Best Actress. Stevens's direction was nearly faultless and his success with this picture began his impressive career. Even today, many film buffs consider *Alice Adams* one of the finest films of the thirties.

OPPOSITE Hepburn in *Sylvia Scarlett,* as a young woman who masquerades as a boy to help her larcenous father flee the country. She and director George Cukor, who had had such success with *A Bill of Divorcement* and *Little Women,* felt that this story, transferred to film, would be their greatest achievement. It is easy to see why the challenge appealed to Kate: it was a chance to show the critics that she could actually *be* a man on screen, instead of just, as they often complained, acting like one.

FOLLOWING PAGES Kate with Brian Aherne as the handsome young artist whom Sylvia meets while still disguised as a boy and for whom she drops her masquerade.

PREVIOUS PAGES Going over the script during a break in filming. The set of *Sylvia Scarlett* was a happy one; Kate and George Cukor were convinced they were making a marvelous picture, and the cast—which also included Cary Grant, in his first comic role—got along well.

Kate is attended to after taking a pounding in the Pacific Ocean. A scene called for Cary Grant to run into the water to rescue a young woman, but the late October waters were frigid, and he refused.

Natalie Paley, the actress in the water, was tiring, and started to call for help. Still, Cary refused. Kate found it all very funny, until Cukor challenged her to rescue Natalie herself. She did so, and both actresses emerged from the water exhausted and trembling with the cold.

During the filming of these beach scenes, Hepburn's new beau flew his biplane onto a landing strip and joined the cast and crew for lunch. Everyone tried not to stare, but it was difficult; Kate's suitor was Howard Hughes. The two staunch individualists saw a great deal of each other during this period, and they had fun swimming, playing golf and tennis and dodging photographers. There were rumors of marriage passed on by a breathless press, but never any real chance of it: by now, Kate had decided never to marry again. Her career was the most important thing in her life.

Kate, Cary Grant, and Edmund Gwenn, who played Sylvia's father. Their expressions were undoubtedly similar after they learned of the public's reaction to *Sylvia Scarlett*. Kate, in fact, witnessed it first hand after agreeing to attend a preview of the film, something she never did—so sure was she that the film would be a smash. She and Cukor toasted themselves at dinner, then entered the theater. The audience reaction was devastating: they booed, yelled at the screen, and began leaving the theater twenty minutes into the picture.

It was a film way ahead of its time; audiences of the 1930s didn't want to watch a woman pretend to be a man unless it was done as total farce. Worse, the sexual ambiguities of Kate's performance and the relationships in the film—of which Hepburn and Cukor were justifiably proud—went over the heads of some audiences and infuriated others.

The film was such a disaster—the New York *Sun* critic called it "a tragic waste of time and screen talent"—that Pandro Berman, who had allowed himself to be talked into it against his better judgment by Kate and Cukor, refused to accept their offer to work for him for free next time to make it up: "I never want to see either of you again!"

"But alas," says Cukor, "he did see us again. Over and over again. He couldn't get rid of us."

OPPOSITE Pandro Berman calmed down and offered Kate a role far more suited to her than Sylvia Scarlett: Mary of Scotland. Kate was intrigued by the star-crossed queen, especially since Mary's second husband, the Earl of Bothwell, was a Hepburn of whom she is a direct descendant.

With Douglas Watson, John Carradine, and Frieda Inescort. During filming, director John Ford saved Kate from an ugly accident, perhaps even saving her life. Riding sidesaddle on a galloping horse in one scene, Kate did not see a large tree branch looming ahead of her. Just in time, Ford screamed at her, "Duck!" She did, and missed the branch by inches.

Mary of Scotland was based upon a play, written in blank verse, by Maxwell Anderson, and it did not translate well to film. Although the dialogue was changed substantially, the film still turned out wordy and static, and the public did not respond to it. As so often before, Kate's reviews were far superior to those of the film. William Boehnel in the New York *World-Telegram* opined, "It is left to Miss Hepburn to bring Mary vividly, glowingly, to life. This she does. To be brief about it, she gives the part nobility. Acting with an unassuming pride, she has the courage and taste to underplay. As a result she suggests grandeur without having to describe it."

There had never been any question in Hollywood that Katharine Hepburn was an accomplished *actress,* but now many wondered whether she had what it takes to remain a *star.* It was obvious that her drawing power at the box office varied greatly depending on the vehicle. Kate could only hope that her next film would turn the tide of box-office flops she found herself caught up in.

The film she chose was *A Woman Rebels,* the saga of a woman's struggle for liberation during the Victorian period. It again afforded Kate the opportunity to play a strong-minded, independent woman; she patterned her performance after her mother's women's rights activities. The picture also gave her the chance to wear no fewer than twenty-two gorgeous Plunkett creations.

Hepburn's stunning costumes in this and most of her previous films were designed by Walter Plunkett, a creative genius whom Hepburn considered part of her "inner circle" and with whom she always preferred to work during the 1930s. "Most actresses," Plunkett says, "think of their wardrobes as costumes. With Kate, her mind accepted them as the things she would normally put on every morning. She studied how they were worn until she was completely comfortable with them."

Kate is caught off guard during filming of *A Woman Rebels*. Whether Depression-era audiences were tired of opulent depictions of wealth on screen, or not quite ready for the women's rights politics of the story, *A Woman Rebels* was still another major financial failure. *Time* magazine addressed itself to the Hepburn dilemma: "Ever since Katharine Hepburn set the cinema industry by the ears with *Little Women,* her employers have been trying doggedly to discover just what elusive factor, added to the stock formula of Lavender and Old Lace, made that picture so sensationally successful. *A Woman Rebels* represents an effort to discover if the element was the revolt of a young girl against convention. That the experiment is conducted with painstaking care only makes it the more apparent that the hypothesis is faulty."

Hepburn had long wanted to return to the stage, but RKO refused to give her the time off. Now, they hoped that a stage hit would help revitalize her sagging career, and agreed to allow her to appear in a version of *Jane Eyre,* with Dennis Hoey. Hepburn wanted a great deal of money to do the role—she "compromised" at more than a thousand dollars a week—but she refused billing above the title. Complimented on her generosity, Kate retorted, "Generous? I just don't want to stick my neck out!"

After New Haven and Boston, the company moved on to Chicago before the anticipated New York open-

ing. When the influential critic Brooks Atkinson of the New York *Times* panned Hepburn and the show even before its New York premiere, Kate, terrified of a repeat of her humiliation over *The Lake,* asked that the New York opening be canceled. It was.

In Chicago, Kate's relationship with Howard Hughes began making headlines. The local papers reported that Hughes had proposed to Hepburn and applied for a marriage license. Neither activity was ever confirmed, but the couple was frequently spotted together, and reporters once held a twenty-four-hour vigil after a man fitting Hughes's description ran into Kate's New York townhouse. They never did see him leave, although they assumed he must have, somehow.

The "romance" aspects of the relationship may have been overstated by the press, but in any event, the couple saw little of each other after the summer of 1937.

ABOVE A portrait released by RKO to promote Kate's appearance in *Jane Eyre*. The failure of that venture left Hepburn depressed and unsettled. She wondered about her own future, felt guilty that she had, on balance, cost her studio and her favorite producer money, instead of making it for them. Perhaps her next film would reach a larger audience, or the one after that.

What Hepburn couldn't know at this point was that her career difficulties, now known primarily to industry insiders, would soon become, in a flurry of unfavorable publicity, a public issue.

Part Three

"BOX-OFFICE POISON"

1937–1940

OPPOSITE With Franchot Tone. The reviews of *Quality Street* were among the worst Hepburn had ever received; several of the notices were almost cruel. Frank Nugent in the New York *Times* wrote, "Such flutterings and jitterings and twitchings, such hand wringings and mouth quiverings, such runnings about and eyebrow raisings have not been seen on a screen in many a moon."

Quality Street was yet another box-office bomb. Stevens: "Here we are in the middle of the Depression . . . and people are supposed to care about a rich girl in crinolines . . . Maybe we thought it was 'escapist fare' or some goddamned thing. Well, the only thing that escaped was our money—down the drain."

The influential Hollywood trade paper *Variety* voiced a concern much of the movie industry shared: "Three short years ago Katharine Hepburn rocketed to screen heights, but a succession of unfortunate selections of material has marooned a competent girl in a bog of box-office frustration. There probably is no one in pictures who needs a real money film as much as this actress."

Pandro Berman stood by Kate, and offered her one of the main roles in an ensemble picture, *Stage Door.* She gladly accepted.

Kate began her next film, *Quality Street,* with high hopes that it would be a hit: it was an opulent period piece, and the director was George Stevens, who had headed up Hepburn's last successful production.

She played Phoebe Throssel, a young Victorian woman romanced by a doctor (Franchot Tone) who is sent off to the Napoleonic Wars before he can propose. In the ten years until his return, Phoebe has turned from a pretty, coquettish girl to a drab, old-maid schoolteacher.

When her former beau fails to recognize her, Phoebe decides to masquerade as her nonexistent, flirtatious young niece in order to win him back.

FOLLOWING PAGES Hepburn has a snack between takes. Once again, she and George Stevens were at each other's throats during the filming. Stevens began the production in a bad humor, since his commitment to this film left him unable to direct *Winterset,* which he still feels could have been his best picture. He became so annoyed at the group of Hepburn friends and advisers gathered around the set each day that he barred them all permanently. Hepburn was aghast, but Stevens stood his ground: "The gang didn't come in after that. Kate was confused by them; their advice was so diverse she didn't know what she was doing . . . she picked out lightweights to think with, and that was a mistake."

Stevens felt that Kate was too influenced by the precious nature of the period and the people in *Quality Street,* and that her performance bordered on the annoying. Much of the public agreed.

PREVIOUS PAGES Most of the starring cast of *Stage Door* (only Ginger Rogers is missing): Left to right, Eve Arden, Kate, Constance Collier, Andrea Leeds, and Lucille Ball. Based on the play by Edna Ferber and George S. Kaufman (who remarked that this version should have been called *Screen Door*), the film was actually wittier and less self-conscious than the play. Kate portrayed Terry Randall, an aristocratic young woman who joins a group of rapier-tongued showgirls at a boardinghouse. Her clipped diction and spouting of Shakespeare do little to endear her to the other girls, especially her wiseacre roommate (Rogers). Without Terry's knowledge, her father arranges for her to get a part for which she is ill prepared, and for which another of the girls, Kaye (Andrea Leeds), has prepared for years. Terry is awful in the part until opening night, when she hears that Kaye has committed suicide. Her distress leads her to act the part brilliantly, and she dedicates her performance to Kaye.

Gregory LaCava directs Kate and Ginger Rogers. Although the plot sounds hokey, *Stage Door* was a bright, sparkling picture, written with tremendous wit and directed with style. LaCava allowed his actresses to interrupt each other, and there is much overlapping of dialogue; several viewings of the film are necessary to catch every witticism.

Kate's playing of Terry Randall was her best work since *Morning Glory*. She and Terry had several parallels: both were rich and overconfident, both had fathers who opposed their acting ambitions yet helped them along; both received leading parts before they were able to handle them. Further, the play in which Terry does so poorly could have been modeled directly after *The Lake*.

The famous "calla lilies" scene. To this day, Katharine Hepburn imitators recite the lines, "The calla lilies are in bloom again. Such a strange flower, suitable for any occasion." In this film Kate says those immortal words again and again as Terry Randall's director tells her she's not reading the lines properly. Opening night, knowing of her friend's suicide, Terry performs the lines, and those following, movingly: "I carried them on my wedding day; now I place them here in memory of something that has died."

It is an indication of Kate's remarkable talent that she is able to recite those lines, after we have heard them again and again to the point of ridicule, in such a way that they touch us.

Kate as Susan Vance, the zany heroine of Howard Hawks's *Bringing Up Baby*—with Baby, a leopard that causes untold trouble. Hepburn had never done a comedy before, but Hawks was confident she would be wonderful. At first, however, her inexperience led her to play the comedy scenes too lightly, laughing as though she *knew* that what she was doing was funny. Hawks explained to her that great comedy springs from people doing absurd things with deadly earnestness. She changed her playing, and the character of Susan Vance became marvelously funny.

Having a leopard on a movie set created some tense moments; special precautions had to be taken not to startle the animal, including wearing resin on one's shoes to avoid a sudden slip. The leopard's trainer told Hepburn to wear perfume, which always made the animal playful. "Miss Hepburn, to my surprise," the trainer commented, "showed no reluctance at working with the leopard . . . I think if Miss Hepburn should ever leave the screen she would make a very good animal trainer."

Cary Grant matched Kate's performance, acting the stuffy paleontologist whom Susan drives to distraction in a perfect deadpan style. Despite the box-office disaster of *Sylvia Scarlett,* Kate had adored working with Grant, and their chemistry in *Bringing Up Baby* helped make it one of the funniest of the 1930s' "screwball" comedies.

OPPOSITE Kate poses as Terry Randall. The public loved everything about *Stage Door:* it was inventive, fresh, witty, and moving; the young actresses in it played off each other brilliantly, and Kate toned herself down to the point where she was acting, not performing, once again. Praise for Hepburn was lavish: "Never has Miss Hepburn been more compelling, more spellbinding"; "Miss Hepburn has never demonstrated more authority as an actress."

Stage Door was a huge hit. Kate and the studio were justifiably proud and relieved, but the triumph wasn't total: *Stage Door* wasn't a "Katharine Hepburn picture"; its success could be laid to many elements other than her box-office draw. Still, it was a ray of sunshine in a career that had become far too overcast, and Kate was ecstatic.

Director Howard Hawks, Cary, and Kate relax between takes. Hepburn liked and respected Hawks, a strong man who was fond of Kate but refused to coddle her. He enjoys telling the story of the time he embarrassed Hepburn in front of the cast and crew in order to get her to stop talking—he had called for "quiet on the set." Mortified, Kate said she wanted to have a word with him, and told him that he was liable to get into trouble with her friends on the set unless he treated her better. With that, Hawks called to an electrician manning a lamp directly above them. "Eddie, if you had a choice of dropping that lamp on Miss Hepburn or me, which would you choose?"

The electrician responded, "Step aside, Mr. Hawks!"

OPPOSITE On the set, Kate is captured with an expression that could well sum up her reaction to ensuing events. Despite the fact that *Bringing Up Baby* was a fast, funny slapstick comedy which showcased several scintillating performances and received excellent reviews—especially for the "new" Hepburn—it failed to find an audience. Perhaps it was too sophisticated, perhaps audiences had had their fill of screwball comedies—this was one of the last of the breed. Whatever the reason for its tepid box office, the film was another Hepburn disappointment.

But it was soon to be more than that; it became the catalyst for her public humiliation. Shortly after the film opened in March of 1938 and it was clear that it would not be a hit, Harry Brandt, president of the Independent Theater Owners of America, took out a full page ad to pronounce Hepburn and several other major stars "box-office poison."

It was an extremely damaging designation for all concerned, and it received enormous national publicity. Hepburn tried to be jocular. "They tell me I'm a has-been," she said at the time. "If I weren't laughing so much, I might cry." She later admitted that it devastated her to walk by a newsstand near her home and see the words in a trade paper headline.

Kate felt it best to leave RKO, and it became easier for her when they offered her the insulting vehicle *Mother Carey's Chickens*. She bought out her contract for two hundred thousand dollars and never looked back.

OPPOSITE With Cary Grant in a scene from *Holiday*. Columbia Pictures, then still a relatively minor film company, was overjoyed when Kate accepted their offer to star in this film version of the Philip Barry play. Kate was equally thrilled with the chance; she had, of course, understudied the role for months on Broadway.

The story revolved around Linda Seton, a New York socialite who is the black sheep of her family. Her sister meets Johnny Case (Grant) and plans to marry him, expecting that he will enter the family banking business. Johnny has other ideas—he wants to take a prolonged "holiday" and travel around the world to find out about life firsthand. Later, he might settle down to working.

Linda loves the idea, and falls in love with Johnny. When it is clear that Johnny and her sister can never be married, Linda joins Johnny on his world holiday.

Hepburn and Doris Nolan as the Seton sisters. After the shooting was completed, director George Cukor threw a party, and Kate screened the test she had done for RKO in 1932, in which she performed a scene from *Holiday*. "I laughed when I saw myself," she says. "I *led* the laughter, and everyone just fell over. I was so terrible. I turned to George and said, 'Oh God, why did you hire me?' "

Hepburn was terrific in *this* version of *Holiday,* and so were her reviews. *Time*'s critic wrote, "By her performance as Linda, Katharine Hepburn seems highly likely to refute the argument . . . that her box-office appeal (is) practically nil. Highly responsive to the cajolings of pudgy, moon-faced director Cukor, she gives her liveliest performance since his *Little Women.*"

Still, *Holiday* wasn't a hit, and the "box-office poison" label wasn't refuted. Hepburn returned home to Connecticut to take stock of her life and career. It would be a year and a half before she returned to the screen.

A rare photograph of Kate with her sisters Peggy (right) and Marion, 1939. Spotting Peggy at a performance of *The Lake* years earlier, Noel Coward quipped, "She looks the way Kate should have, but didn't."

On March 28, 1939, Hepburn opens in a Philip Barry play written especially for her, *The Philadelphia Story*. Kate, in fact, made quite a few "suggestions" about the play after finding the second and third acts weak, and some observers feel she deserved "co-author" status. The story was a thin one: Tracy Lord, a society girl, is set to marry a Philadelphia Main Liner when her drunken ex-husband arrives on the scene with a reporter and photographer from *Spy* magazine, all set to record the nuptials. Tracy has an aversion to the press and refuses to allow them to cover the wedding—until they tell her that unless she does, they will print a story about her father's affair with an actress.

Comic situations ensue, including Tracy's beginning to fall for the reporter. At play's end, she remarries her first husband.

With Joseph Cotton as Tracy's first husband. A great deal rode on the success of *The Philadelphia Story*—for the playwright, for the Theater Guild which presented it and, especially, for Kate. Financing was difficult to come by for a group of creative people with few hits to count among their recent productions. Kate and Barry each agreed to put up a quarter of the costs, the Guild came up with a quarter—and a silent partner, Howard Hughes, put up the rest. Kate took little salary, but was guaranteed 10 percent of the Broadway gross, 12½ percent of any road grosses, and rights to make the play into a movie.

ABOVE RIGHT With Dan Tobin as the *Spy* reporter. Throughout rehearsals and tryouts, Kate was terrified that *The Philadelphia Story* would be another debacle for her. Barry, a friend, was appalled at the highly mannered playing of all the principals and began screaming at them one day during a rehearsal. Kate told him to butt out. Another time, Kate was performing what she thought was a serious scene to an out-of-town audience, which began laughing. She thought they hated it, but later realized she should play the scene for laughs.

Kate was so sure she was headed for disaster again that she begged the producers not to open in New York. They refused. Opening night, she insisted that the curtain go up with her already on stage so she would not be thrown off by the audience's reaction to her first appearance, and she kept muttering under her breath, "This is Indianapolis, this is Indianapolis" so that the pressures of a New York opening wouldn't get to her.

The Philadelphia Story was a total triumph; all the script problems were worked out, Kate's mannerisms were toned down, audiences loved her and the play. For the first time, there was mention in the press of the stuff Kate Hepburn was made of: Richard Watts of the *Herald Tribune* wrote, "Few actresses have been so relentlessly assailed by critics, wits, columnists, magazine editors and other professional assailants over so long a period of time, and even if you confess that some of the abuse had a certain amount of justification to it, you must admit she faced it gamely and unflinchingly and fought back with courage and gallantry."

The Philadelphia Story grossed over one and a half million dollars, and made Katharine Hepburn even richer than she already was. But most important to her was the fact that she controlled the film rights—and she wasn't going to let the picture be made without her. She would return to Hollywood, she vowed, and show them something about box office!

Hepburn with artist McClelland Barclay in his studio, June 15, 1939. She posed for his painting "The Spirit of Tolerance," which was made into a poster to promote the upcoming Independence Day Ceremonies by the national Council Against Intolerance in America.

OPPOSITE Katharine Hepburn returns to Hollywood: Kate and Jimmy Stewart in the film version of *The Philadelphia Story*. Several movie studios were interested in the vehicle, but only MGM was willing to make it with Hepburn as Tracy. She told MGM head Louis B. Mayer that she wanted to "protect" herself against box-office failure by having two of MGM's biggest stars—Spencer Tracy and Clark Gable—play opposite her. Mayer blanched, knowing that neither would accept; both male roles were decidedly secondary to Hepburn's. Mayer offered Jimmy Stewart, a rising new star whose contract gave him no choice in the matter. Hepburn admired his work and approved him. Mayer had no suggestions for the other actor, but gave Hepburn $150,000 to hire anyone she wanted.

She approached Cary Grant, who had one condition—he was to receive top billing. Kate, who has never cared much about things like that, agreed.

Kate poses for a costume test. She looked particularly lovely in this film, and she gave most of the credit to cinematographer Joseph Ruttenberg. After filming was completed, she sent a note and gift to him: "Dear Joe, I hope my long thin throat has not driven you to drink. But if you please, I hope that these [cut glass decanters] will give you strength to think of that long string bean you made a queen. [Signed] The new glamorous Katrink."

OPPOSITE TOP Tracy takes a dip in the pool. *The Philadelphia Story* set was a happy one; Kate felt especially at home with Cary Grant and director George Cukor. Kate and Cukor clashed only a few times, once, ironically, when Kate wanted to cry and Cukor thought it would be better if she didn't (she had evidently changed her mind about such matters since *Alice Adams*). Cukor was much impressed by Hepburn's performance: "She was perfect as Tracy Lord—she was arrogant but sensitive, she was tough, but vulnerable, she didn't care what people thought of her, they had to accept her on her own terms, or forget it. Of course, she was far more polished, more skillful, than she had ever been before."

OPPOSITE BOTTOM With Jimmy Stewart and Cary Grant in the climactic wedding scene. Attempting an explanation of Kate's prior unpopularity, George Cukor remarked, "She challenged the audience and that wasn't the fashion in those days. When people first saw her they saw something arrogant in her playing."

This was true as well of Tracy Lord, but there was a difference: Tracy comes to realize that she is too arrogant, too cold; at the end of the film she has become a warm, yielding woman. The audiences of the day loved it, and they loved Hepburn for it. *The Philadelphia Story* was a smash hit, the biggest in Kate's career, and it was decidedly her own triumph this time. Suddenly, she was no longer "box-office poison," but—in her own words—"Top of the Heap."

Kate received a Best Actress nomination for the film but lost to Ginger Rogers in *Kitty Foyle*. Jimmy Stewart and the film's screenplay won Oscars.

Hepburn lunches with President Franklin Roosevelt as his son Elliott serves chowder. In typical Hepburn fashion, she became involved in a misadventure on her way to the President's Hyde Park residence on the Hudson River in New York.

A friend flew her to a landing strip near the residence, and Kate began walking toward the house. She got caught in mud, then was stopped by a guard who told her she couldn't go any further. After she convinced him that she was an invited guest, the guard let her proceed. As she stopped at a stream to wash the mud off her feet and shoes, she was spotted by the President, as he drove past her in his car. Roosevelt found Kate's explanation highly amusing.

A 1941 portrait of Kate. She was now in her early thirties, and her beauty had taken on a lustrous womanliness it had only hinted at before. In the early forties, Katharine Hepburn's beauty was truly unsurpassed.

As the decade began, Kate was about to enter a new and thrilling phase of her career, and her life: she met Spencer Tracy.

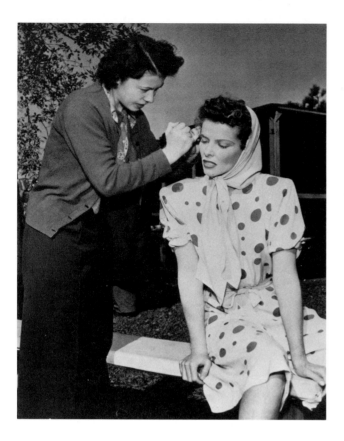

Hepburn is attended to by hairdresser Irma Wergerer on the set of *Without Love*. This film version was far more successful than the stage presentation, both artistically and financially. Tracy was the foil for Hepburn that Elliott Nugent had not been, and audiences found the film funny and enjoyable. It was now clear to everyone that the Tracy/Hepburn team was an enduringly potent cinema force.

OPPOSITE In strong profile, Robert Mitchum menaces Hepburn and Robert Taylor in this publicity shot for *Undercurrent*. Kate's twenty-second film revolved around a young girl who is led by her new husband (Taylor) to believe that his brother (Mitchum) is a psychopath; she soon learns that her worst suspicions are true: it is her husband, not his brother, who is mentally deranged.

PREVIOUS PAGES Tracy, Hepburn, and friend in a charming publicity still for *Without Love*. The film's director, Harold Bucquet, found that "directing Mr. Tracy amounts to telling him when you're ready to start a scene. He hasn't let me down yet, and if he does, perhaps we'll get acquainted. Miss Hepburn requires direction, for she tends to act too much. Her acting is much less economical than Mr. Tracy's but his style is rubbing off on her."

In their personal life, *her* style was rubbing off on *him:* she had, by this time, convinced him to stop drinking. Despite her abhorrence of alcoholism, she had stuck by him through his worst binges, sometimes having to find him and bring him home in the middle of the night. But she had accomplished her goal of making him sober a little too late: by the time he stopped drinking, his health, and particularly his liver, had seriously deteriorated.

On the set, Robert Taylor mocks Kate's habit of walking around between scenes with her hair wrapped in a towel.

Despite the fact that *Undercurrent* was a tense melodrama, the mood on the set appears to have been light. Here, Kate inspects a barrel given to her after she complained that there was no convenient place she could swim during filming. The sign behind her reads: "Katy's swimming hole—hang your clothes on the hickory limb."

Undercurrent was directed by Vincente Minnelli, one of MGM's top directors, who usually did musicals. Hepburn befriended him and his wife, Judy Garland, and attempted to help Garland with her personal problems. She encouraged Judy to take morning walks to relieve her insomnia in the hope that she could be weaned from sleeping pills, and in 1950, after a highly publicized Garland suicide attempt, Hepburn visited her every day, her spunk and humor helping Judy to get back on her feet.

In her trailer, Kate looks over her fan mail between scenes. *Undercurrent* was not a success; as so often before, Hepburn's notices were far better than the film's. Howard Barnes in the New York *Herald Tribune:* "The valid reasons for witnessing *Undercurrent* are all contained in the performing. Miss Hepburn handles (her role) with skill and a variety of expression which does her great credit. Either as a bobby soxer or a curious *femme fatale,* she gives a resounding portrayal."

Always ready to try anything, Kate is helped onto an antique bicycle for a ride around the studio lot during filming of *Sea of Grass.*

FOLLOWING PAGES A scene from *Sea of Grass,* in which Spencer and Kate played a cattle tycoon and his wife. Although it was filmed before *Undercurrent,* it was not released until three months after that film, on February 27, 1947.

March 22, 1947: Kate and Jimmy Stewart perform a "Screen Guild of the Air" presentation of *The Philadelphia Story*.

During rehearsals for the radio performance of *The Philadelphia Story,* Cary Grant makes fun of Kate's penchant for wearing pants by slipping on a plaid skirt and pulling up his pants leg. Not to be outdone, Kate takes off her socks, saying that there are too many girls in bobby socks swooning over Grant.

FOLLOWING PAGES Kate as Clara Wieck Schumann in *Song of Love,* the melodramatic version of the true story of Clara's marriage to composer Robert Schumann.

OPPOSITE Kate with the uncredited child actress who played her young daughter in *Sea of Grass.* The film was not a pleasant experience for anyone concerned. Director Elia Kazan, who had made just one film, *A Tree Grows in Brooklyn,* was dismayed to learn that the film would be shot on the studio lot, not on location. "To my vast humiliation," he says, "I never saw a blade of grass through that picture." Kazan, something of a Method director, was unable to relate to his stars. He was intimidated by Kate and felt excluded from the Tracy/Hepburn inner circle. He was not comfortable with Tracy's reported theory of acting: "Learn your lines and don't bump into the furniture." Tracy considered the Method emphasis on motivation and "sense

memory" ridiculous mumbo-jumbo; star and director did not communicate too well.

Kazan had envisioned *Sea of Grass* as "like a Russian picture, you should have almost smelled the land." Instead, it turned into a glossy MGM epic in which, as one participant said anonymously, "every time Kate went to the bathroom, she came back in a new costume."

Whether or not the public would have responded to the picture Kazan wanted to make, they did not like this one at all. The reviews—for the film, Spencer *and* Kate—were terrible, and it is considered by most the least appealing of the Tracy/Hepburn movies.

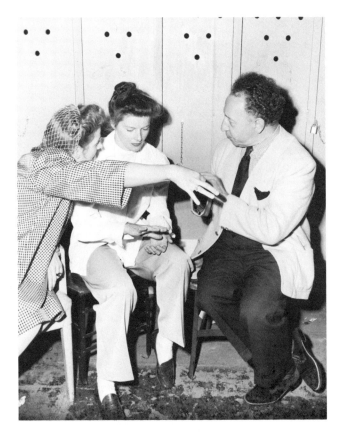

Maestro Artur Rubinstein and his wife explain to Kate the importance of hand flexibility in piano playing. Producer-director Clarence Brown had told Kate that she needed merely to fake piano playing while Rubinstein played the Schumann, Brahms, and Liszt compositions on the piano. Hepburn snorted, "Nonsense! I'm not going to pound away at some goddamned keyboard. I'm going to play a real piano. Rubinstein can carry the bulk of the works, but I'm going to lead in with the first few bars, and I'll bet nobody knows the difference."

No one did, either. Here, Kate studies with Rubinstein protégée Laura Dubman. In three weeks, she had learned to play well enough that even Rubinstein was astounded. "If I hadn't seen it and heard it with my own eyes and ears, I wouldn't have believed it! That woman is incredible. She actually does play almost as well as I do. And when she ends and I begin, only I in the whole world could tell the difference!"

OPPOSITE Hepburn relaxes between scenes. She was, it seemed, capable of doing almost anything, except guaranteeing that her films would be hits. Once again, with the lukewarm public reaction to *Song of Love,* Kate was in the midst of a string of box-office disappointments. This time, however, there was no thought on her part of leaving her studio. She loved working at MGM, where she was treated as royalty, given practically anything she wanted, and well protected from the privacy invasions of the press. Reportedly, Garson Kanin once asked her, "How can you stay at that studio? They're giving you such lousy parts and such stinking pictures."

"Oh, yes," Kate replied. "But they're marvelous when you come through Chicago, and have to change trains."

State of the Union, the 1948 Frank Capra film, featured Spencer and Kate as a presidential candidate and his estranged wife. She at first pretends they are still happily married in order to bolster his chances, then realizes that he has sold out his principles for ambition and convinces him to withdraw from the race.

The part of the wife was originally supposed to be played by Claudette Colbert, but a few days before shooting began, she told Capra that she was unwilling to work after 5 P.M. Unable to accept this stipulation, Capra fired her, and asked Tracy if he knew anyone who could fill in on the spur of the moment. He did.

Kate proudly shows Frank Capra the cake in the form of a lamb given to her with affection by the *State of the Union* crew. Hepburn needed all the support she could get at this time; the House Un-American Activities Committee was close to launching an investigation into her liberal attitudes and activities.

Kate was aghast at the archconservative committee's smear campaign against many of her colleagues; in some cases it appeared that not being conservative was enough to have some politician label you a Communist. Kate stood up to the committee and the witch-hunters in a statement: "J. Parnell Thomas, head of the House Un-American Committee, engages in a personally conducted smear campaign of the motion picture industry. He is aided and abetted in this effort by a group of super-patriots who call themselves the Motion Picture Alliance for the Preservation of American Ideals. For myself, I want no part of their ideals or those of Mr. Thomas . . . The artist, since the beginning of time, has always expressed the aspirations and dreams of his people. Silence the artist and you have silenced the most articulate voice the people have."

On June 5, 1948, six weeks after the New York opening of *State of the Union,* Kate sails to Paris on the SS *Nieuw Amsterdam* for a vacation.

FOLLOWING PAGES Spencer was equally disdainful of the Red Scare campaign, but he kept his own counsel. He never believed that actors should get involved in politics. "Remember who shot Lincoln," he was fond of saying.

State of the Union had enough of a political message anyway. It was moderately successful at the box office, and went far toward reviving the careers of Tracy and Hepburn. The reviews were good; Howard Barnes in the New York *Herald Tribune* wrote, "With (Tracy's) forthright acting and his knowledge of the nuances which make a screen scene click, he brings a satirical and very human account of political skulduggery into sharp focus. Aiding and abetting him no end is Katharine Hepburn. She is restrained, persuasive and altogether delightful . . . *State of the Union* is a triumphant film, marked all over by Frank Capra's artistry."

In Paris, Kate shares wine and chips with Clark Gable. Although both were MGM stars, they never worked together.

Spencer as Adam Bonner and Kate as Amanda Bonner in *Adam's Rib*. Probably the best-loved of the Tracy/Hepburn films, it was inspired by an idea of Ruth Gordon's which she and her husband, Garson Kanin, developed into a screenplay: what would happen if two lawyers, married to each other, wind up on opposing sides of a court case?

PREVIOUS PAGES *Adam's Rib,* which opened in December 1949, was a smash success for Tracy and Hepburn, and a much-needed shot in the arm for the financially troubled MGM. The script was fast and funny, Spencer and Kate were at their best, and they were supported brilliantly by David Wayne, Tom Ewell, Jean Hagan, and, especially, Judy Holliday.

Bosley Crowther in the New York *Times* wrote: "(Mr. Tracy and Miss Hepburn's) perfect compatibility in comic capers is delightful to see. A line thrown away, a lifted eyebrow, a smile or a sharp, resounding slap on a tender part of the anatomy is as natural as breathing to them. Plainly, they took great pleasure in playing this rambunctious spoof."

OPPOSITE On location for a "home-movie" sequence in *Adam's Rib*. Many filmgoers thought they were seeing actual footage of Kate and Spencer "at home" in this sequence. Indeed, many of the exchanges and situations between the Bonners were based on fact; the Kanins modeled their characters after their close friends.

For the entire length of his relationship with Katharine Hepburn, Spencer Tracy was, of course, married to another woman. By all appearances, Mrs. Tracy was extraordinarily understanding of the situation. Accepting of the fact that the kind of marriage she had once shared with Spencer was over, and because her church forbade divorce, she made the best of it, and did not stand in the way of Kate and Spencer's relationship.

In fact, Katharine Hepburn and Louise Tracy shared a bond of affection and concern for Spencer which would later result in an extraordinary scene: the two women taking turns sitting by Spencer's bedside during an illness.

Kate and William Prince in the Broadway production of *As You Like It,* January 1950. Hepburn was terrified of playing Shakespeare, but typically she decided to take the role of Rosalind for just that reason: "I realize I'm putting my head on the line," she said at the time. "But for me, the personal satisfaction justifies the risk . . . the part of Rosalind is really a good test of how good an actress you are, and I want to find out." Kate asked Constance Collier, a close friend since *Stage Door,* to coach her, and Miss Collier attended every performance, watching Kate through opera glasses.

Hepburn acquitted herself quite well. Audiences loved the energy and grace she brought to the part, and much was made of her legs, which she had rarely revealed previously. Some critics felt Kate was still more Bryn Mawr than Stratford-on-Avon, but the reviews were generally good and the show went on to present 145 performances.

OPPOSITE Judy Garland, Billie Burke, and Kate admire a portrait of Ethel Barrymore at Miss Barrymore's seventieth birthday party, late 1950.

On March 17, 1951, Kate's mother died in her sleep at the family home in Hartford. She was seventy-three. Kate was hit hard by the loss of this woman she loved and admired so much. She took some solace in the fact that her mother, who loved Shakespeare, had been able to see her play Rosalind.

Kate consoled herself with plans to return to movies. She received a marvelous script, *The African Queen,* to be directed by John Huston and to co-star Humphrey Bogart. She immediately accepted the assignment.

The halcyon days of the Tracy-Hepburn screen partnership ended with the 1940s. Over the next seventeen years, although their personal relationship remained as strong as ever, they would make just three more films together. Both managed admirably on their own, however. Indeed, over the next two decades, Katharine Hepburn would make some of the finest films of her career.

Part Five

SURVIVOR

1951–1966

OPPOSITE Hepburn meets Bogart. The formidable pair were teamed by director John Huston for the film version of C. S. Forester's novel *The African Queen*. The story of a haughty missionary spinster and a hard-drinking riverboat captain and their unlikely teaming to escape a dangerous Africa at the beginning of World War I, the vehicle was a perfect one for these two Hollywood veterans.

At first, Kate drove Bogie crazy, exactly as prim Rose Sayer did Captain Allnut. "Here is either a twenty-four-carat nut or a great actress working mighty hard at being one," Bogie said. "You wait for the laughs [you were] promised, but you can't stand the dame. She won't let anybody get a word in edgewise and keeps repeating what a superior person she is . . . Later you get a load of the babe stalking through an African jungle as though she had beaten Livingstone to it. . . . She pounces on the flora and fauna with a home movie camera like a kid seeing his first Christmas tree, and she blunders within ten feet of a wild boar's tusks for a close-up of the beast. About every other minute she wrings her hands in ecstasy and says, 'What divine natives! What divine morning glories!' Brother, your brow goes up . . . is this something from *The Philadelphia Story?*"

But Bogart and his wife Lauren Bacall (who accompanied him to the location) became great friends with Kate. Even his opinion of her looks changed. At first, when director John Huston told Bogie about Kate's comment that "plain women know more about men than beautiful ones do," Bogart replied, "Since she's a crow, she should know." After filming, he said, "I found that no one is sexier than Katie, especially before a movie camera, and you remember she has legs like Dietrich . . . You learn to brand as rank slander the crack that you can throw a hat at Katie and it'll hang wherever it hits."

ABOVE With John Huston on location in Africa. Huston and Bogie took great joy in teasing Kate. They would make a show of drinking straight Scotch in front of her, and delight in telling lewd Irish jokes. Finally Kate made the portentous comment, "You boys believe you're being awfully wicked, don't you? Well, you don't know what the word wicked means!"

Kate came to feel that perhaps her co-star and director had the right idea: "I was so busy complaining about Bogey and John drinking hard liquor I tried to shame them by drinking water in their presence at mealtimes. Well, the water was full of germs! They never got sick, and I had the Mexican trots and was in bed every day for weeks! I thought I was going to die—and in the Belgian Congo!"

As with Bogie, Kate became quite fond of Huston. He related in his autobiography, "I remember the many nights I sat with Kate on the top deck of the paddle-boat and watched the eyes of the hippos in the water all around us; every eye seemed to be staring in our direction. And we talked, we talked about nothing and everything. But there was never an idea of romance—Spencer Tracy was the only man in Kate's life."

Kate makes a quick change in her jungle "dressing room." At first, she had insisted on a private changing room, and it was built on a boat that was pulled along the river by the *African Queen,* along with two others carrying camera equipment. The *African Queen,* however, couldn't handle towing all three, so Katie's dressing room had to go. From then on, it was all improvisation. As Lauren Bacall remembered, "The woods was our loo and Katie and I would trudge out as the spirit moved us, standing watch for each other."

In July 1951, the production was forced to return to London after three grueling months in Africa. Filming *The African Queen* was a horror for everyone. It was hot and humid, there were insects everywhere. Most of the crew came down with some malady or other, including malaria and dysentery. Everyone slept in grass huts, the legs of their beds sitting in cans of kerosene so that bugs and scorpions couldn't climb in with them.

One day, Kate and Lauren went back to their tents and ran out screaming. Thousands of ants—huge black flesh-eaters—had invaded their campsite, covering the floors, clothing, everything. There was no way to get rid of them, and the campsite had to be abandoned.

ABOVE RIGHT A rather startling advertisement for *The African Queen,* in which Kate is made to look more like Gina Lollobrigida than Rose Sayer. The studio ob-

viously wasn't sure the public would respond to this unorthodox love story between an older man and woman, and decided to play up the sex and action angles.

They needn't have bothered. *The African Queen* turned out to be one of the biggest money-makers of 1952 and has remained one of America's best-loved films.

It also marked the emergence of Katharine Hepburn as a genuine screen great. She was unafraid, at forty-four, to act a haggard fifty-five-year-old spinster, and she did it brilliantly, bringing a vulnerability and openness to Rose that made her, ultimately, as accessible to audiences as the easier-to-identify-with Allnut.

The film was a triumph for all concerned, especially Hepburn and Bogart. John Huston's observations about his actors echoed the reviewers' sentiments: "Bogie and Katie expanded as actors. They were both playing roles strictly against type, and for me they were a revelation. The spontaneity, the instinctive subtle interplay between them, the way they climbed inside of the people they were supposed to be—all of this made it better than we had written it, as human, as comprehending as we had any right to expect from any two actors."

In April 1952, Humphrey Bogart won his only Academy Award, for *The African Queen.* Kate had been nominated, but lost to Vivien Leigh's extraordinary Blanche DuBois in *A Streetcar Named Desire.* "No one does it alone," Bogie said on accepting the award. "John and Katie helped me to be where I am now."

Hepburn as Epifania, the spoiled, zany heiress of *The Millionairess,* March 1952. Kate had long wanted to do a Shaw play. "My mother worshiped Shaw," Kate said. "She knew everything he'd ever written. Backwards. So did my father. A great deal of Shaw was read aloud at home."

It is easy to see why the part appealed to Kate: Epifania is a whirlwind character, a wildly energetic woman who challenges her suitors to judo matches. Kate's gusto in the part enthralled the London critics, whose praise of Hepburn turned the show into a huge success. Characteristically, Hepburn pooh-poohed the personal superlatives. "I think it went over so well here," she told a British reporter, "because American vitality has a great appeal for the British. But back home, vitality is not so bloody unique."

She may have been right—when the show was brought to the Shubert Theater on Broadway, its ten-week run barely broke even. Still, she enjoyed playing Epifania so much she bought the screen rights, worked for months with writer Preston Sturges on a screenplay, and tried to interest a studio in the project. She was unsuccessful. For one of the few times in her life, she was forced to admit defeat. "Certainly the greatest disappointment of my life," she called it. "I still read the script today. It's just wonderful."

With Australian actor Robert Helpmann in a scene from *The Millionairess.* Helpmann played the Egyptian doctor who challenges and wins Epifania. If Helpmann's authorized biography is to be believed, he would have liked to have won Katharine, too. He described Hepburn as "the only person in my whole life with whom I could be from morning till night and not be bored; the only person I can imagine being married to."

Helpmann jumped to Kate's defense when her attempts to save her voice from encroaching laryngitis led to press reports that she wasn't speaking to any of the crew members. "Of all the people in the theater who like and admire Kate," he said, "the stagehands probably head the list. She has no airs of any kind and for that they love her."

Kate remained fast friends with Robert Helpmann, and they worked together again, but there never was a chance for romance. She and "the only man in Kate's life," Spencer Tracy, were about to make another film together.

Kate as athlete Pat Pemberton in *Pat and Mike*. When Hepburn returned from *African Queen* locations, she saw that Spencer, depressed by her absence and the House Un-American Activities Committee's hearings, had begun drinking heavily again. She was helped considerably in her efforts to get Spence back on the wagon when they began to work on a new Garson Kanin/Ruth Gordon script about an athlete and her manager. With George Cukor directing, it promised to be a pleasant experience, and it was.

The film was a good choice for Kate at this point in her life; it gave her a chance to be athletic on screen and show off her prowess in a variety of sports. More important, it gave her a chance to show audiences that she hadn't *really* aged prematurely: she looked a lot better than she did in *The African Queen*.

The sports sequences gave Kate another opportunity to display her legs, and her skimpy outfits inspired one of the film's best lines. Garson Kanin had written a comment for Spencer to say in appreciation of Kate— "She's really stacked."

When it was agreed that *stacked* wasn't exactly what Kate was, Kanin came up with another line: "There ain't much meat on her, but what there is, is cherce!"

It was a marvelous description, delivered with a twinkle by Spencer, and it got one of the film's biggest laughs.

Tennis star Frank Parker goes over court form with Hepburn as George Cukor looks on. Although an accomplished golf and tennis player, Kate took coaching from top professionals in the field in order to make completely realistic her portrayal of a professional sportswoman.

OPPOSITE Kate and Spencer relax between shots. *Pat and Mike* developed into one of the best of the Tracy/Hepburn comedies; both were at the top of their form, and their interplay had been polished to near perfection. The film was a big hit, both commercially and critically.

Pat and Mike, released in June 1952, was the last film for Kate on her MGM contract.

Kate as Jane Hudson in David Lean's film *Summertime,* based on the stage play by Arthur Laurents.

In order to make *Summertime,* Kate had to leave Spencer once again, but the part was too good to resist. She plays a middle-aged spinster who fulfills a lifelong dream by visiting Venice. While there, she meets and has a whirlwind romance with a handsome, dashing antiques dealer (Rossano Brazzi). When she learns he is married, she returns home to resume the life she left, a sadder but somehow more complete woman.

In *Summertime*'s most famous sequence, Jane gets too close to a canal while taking pictures and falls in with a great splash.

Although Kate was enchanted with the beauty and antiquity of Venice, she was quite appalled by its filth—and nothing in the city was dirtier than its canals. Aware that she would have to fall into the water—and refusing a stand-in—Kate took considerable precautions against infection. She was still occasionally weak from the dysentery she had contracted in Africa, and she didn't want a repeat. She rinsed her mouth with disinfectant, put Vaseline on her skin and a special pomade on her hair, and wore shoes that wouldn't waterlog.

She forgot about her eyes, however, and when she emerged from the canal they were inflamed and runny. They became infected—incurably, it turned out—and to this day Kate's eyes water almost continuously. "When people ask me why I cry such a lot in pictures," Kate has said, "I say, mysteriously, 'Canal in Venice.'"

Kate's performance in *Summertime* was a sublime accomplishment. She conveyed perfectly the childlike enthusiasm of a woman in a romantic city, her rush into a fantasy affair, and her resigned stoicism when reality intervened. Kate loved the film, and so did much of the public—it became her fifth big hit in a row when it opened in June 1955.

By now, Hepburn's art was becoming the subject of intellectual discourse. Lee Rogosin offered this assessment of Kate's latest performance in *Saturday Review:* "Miss Hepburn has labored long in the service of her art and, like many grand actress personalities, she has now created herself in her own image. Everything superfluous is gone, the elements are refined and complete—the sad mouth, the headback laugh, the snap of *chic* in shirtmaker dresses, the dream of enchantment behind wistful eyes, the awakened puritan passion of the girl in love, the 'regular' way with children, the leggy stride, and always the bones—the magnificent, prominent, impossible bones which a visiting journalist [Art Buchwald], made somewhat exuberant by the deceptively mild local wine, described as 'the greatest calcium deposit since the white cliffs of Dover.' "

Kate received a Best Actress nomination for this film; Anna Magnani won the award for *The Rose Tattoo.*

March 1955, Kate and Robert Helpmann rehearse *The Taming of the Shrew* in London in preparation for a tour of Australia.

Hepburn joined the famed Old Vic company in a tour of three Shakespeare plays (the others were *Measure for Measure* and *The Merchant of Venice*), each co-starring Hepburn and Helpmann. When she arrived in Australia, Hepburn gave a rare press conference at which her responses were typically insouciant. Asked about her less-than-glamorous attire, she replied, "Dorothy Gish once made a remark that sums up everything I feel about dress. She observed, 'I'm paid to dress up on my working hours. Why should I bother in my free time?' "

The Sydney leg of the tour was a huge success, but a Melbourne newspaper got things off on the wrong foot in that city on the very first day. Kate recalls a front-page article which read "We have no idea why Miss Hepburn chose to come to Melbourne, except that it was quite obvious her career must be over as a motion picture star."

Despite such ungallantry, Kate was enraptured by all of Australia. Typically, she thirsted to see as much of it as possible, taking Helpmann along. He had never seen much of his own country, and certainly not with the enthusiasm of this visitor. "It is thrilling to discover a new country," he said. "But it is even more thrilling to discover your own."

The tour, on balance, was a success—and Kate would do Shakespeare again, in the United States.

With Burt Lancaster in a rather campy publicity still for *The Rainmaker*. Kate did not get along well with Lancaster; their acting styles clashed, and he never completely believed in the script. But there was no animosity between them, and Kate, with her usual generosity, agreed to his receiving top billing, even though she was the more important star at that point in their careers.

Despite the character's similarities to Jane Hudson, Kate succeeded in creating an original individual in Lizzie Curry. Her performance was praised when the film was released in December 1956. Alton Cook of the New York *World-Telegram* wrote, "Miss Hepburn is superb as she brings elderly, barren despair to a blossoming of radiant, girlish bliss . . ."

The film was moderately successful at the box office, and brought Kate her seventh Oscar nomination. This time, Ingrid Bergman was the winner for *Anastasia*.

Kate as Vinka Kovelenko, Russian airwoman, and Bob Hope as American flier Chuck Lockwood in *The Iron Petticoat*. Kate was intrigued by this farce, inspired by Garbo's *Ninotchka*, about a Communist woman who succumbs to the enticements of capitalism, and she was challenged by the prospect of working with Hope.

Kate chose a novice director, Ralph Thomas, because she had thought his film *Doctor in the House* very funny. Thomas found himself in the middle of chaos. "I wish I had made the picture when I was a little more experienced," he has said, "because of the problem of handling these very diverse personalities. Really, they were playing in two different pictures; she was a mistress of light, sophisticated, romantic comedy, he was much broader, and eventually I didn't so much direct the picture as watch them in action, with a strong bias in her favor."

OPPOSITE Kate as Lizzie Curry in the film version of the Broadway play *The Rainmaker*. Lizzie, a hardworking spinster in a small midwestern town, was something of a cornbelt Jane Hudson, and the story line wasn't all that different from *Summertime:* Lizzie's parched soul is awakened by a traveling con man who introduces her to the wonders of love and sex.

Vinka makes her transition into a glamorous party-goer. *The Iron Petticoat* proved a total disaster for Kate when it opened in New York in February 1957. Screenwriter Ben Hecht, who asked that his name be removed from the credits, felt that his comedy script was destroyed by Bob Hope's gag writers, who kept adding material designed to allow Hope to do what he does best. Hecht took out an ad in *The Hollywood Reporter:* "Although her magnificent comic performance has been blow-torched out of the film, there is enough left of the Hepburn footage to identify her for her sharpshooters. I am assured by my hopeful predators that *The Iron Petticoat* will go over big with people 'who can't get enough of Bob Hope.' "

Some of the reviews were funnier than the film. William K. Zinsser in the New York *Herald Tribune* wrote, " 'Vy you are smilink?' Katharine Hepburn asks Bob Hope, trying her best to sound like a Russian, in *The Iron Petticoat*. Nobody's smilink. In fact, for Hepburn and Hope fans, this should be a day of cryink."

After five years, Tracy and Hepburn are reunited on screen in *Desk Set*. It was a terrific vehicle for them—Tracy plays an electronics engineer who invents a computer which Hepburn fears will take over her job.

Kate was overjoyed to be working again with Spencer, who was having considerable difficulties. He had been drinking, his health was deteriorating. He had been fired from the film *Tribute to a Bad Man* after he disappeared on a binge for a week and broke down before the cameras when he returned. Kate was then in Australia, unable to do anything to help. Two other films which Tracy did complete, *The Mountain* and *The Old Man and the Sea,* proved particularly grueling experiences for him.

But now, Kate was back to nurse Spencer, buck him up, cajole him into working to his greatest potential. At first he didn't want to do *Desk Set,* and she was reluctant to push him too hard. Finally, he was convinced by everyone involved in the project that the movie couldn't be made without him. When he nodded his agreement, tears welled up in Kate's eyes.

Kate clowns around between scenes. The filming was a happy experience for everyone; both Kate and Spencer were pleased with the progress of filming and their performances. As usual, Kate had her fingers in every pie, and a classic Hepburn story emerged from *Desk Set* filming. A large vine was referred to in the script as a philodendron, and Kate said that the plant on the set was not a philodendron. Director Walter Lang told Kate to shut up and go home—it *was so* a philodendron. She insisted, and the prop man was called in. He said it was a philodendron, as did the studio gardener.

Finally, Kate stormed out, yelling, "I'll show you what a philodendron is. You're a bunch of idiots!"

She returned with a plant so large it couldn't fit into the elevator; she had to drag it up the stairs. She pulled it over to Lang and said, *"That* is a philodendron." The gardener admitted he had been wrong and the plant was replaced.

Desk Set was a pleasant, funny picture, with Tracy and Hepburn at the top of their form. Bosley Crowther commented, "Best of all, there are Miss Hepburn and Mr. Tracy. They can tote phone books on their heads or balance feathers on their chins and be amusing— which is about the size of what they do here. Under Walter Lang's relaxed direction, they lope through this trifling charade like a couple of oldtimers who enjoy reminiscing with simple routines."

Desk Set was moderately successful, but it marked the last time Kate and Spencer would work together for ten years.

Hepburn checks her hair minutes before going on stage as Portia in *The Merchant of Venice,* which opened on July 10, 1957. Kate agreed to star in the productions of the struggling American Shakespeare Festival in Stratford, Connecticut for a mere $350 a week. Director John Houseman recalled that she was generous with everyone, a total professional. "She (was) not at all the lady star condescending to lend her presence to us. Rather, she was almost a Girl Scout cheerleader, the chief of the boosters . . . she was kind, thoughtful, generous to the other players. She never upstaged the young girls or pushed them out of the limelight. She was always present thirty minutes before everyone else, and always last to leave."

FOLLOWING PAGES Morris Carnovsky as Shylock, Kate as Portia in *The Merchant of Venice.* John Houseman commented, "She had learned from Constance Collier that the actress must have one major scene in which she justifies the description of 'star.' In *The Merchant of Venice* it was the court scene, and she acted it very finely."

February 25, 1958, Kate gets a good laugh from the outfits worn by members of the Harvard University Hasty Pudding Theatrical Group as they present her with their "Woman of the Year" Award in Cambridge, Massachusetts.

A press photographer captures a rare smile from Hepburn as she is driven from London airport after arriving for a brief vacation in England and Italy, May 1958. Kate hadn't worked for more than eight months, and she wouldn't do another film for almost a year. Most of her time was spent caring for Spencer, and she gave much thought to retiring permanently from films.

PREVIOUS PAGES With Alfred Drake in *Much Ado About Nothing,* the second production of the 1957 summer season. Drake's opinion of Kate differed considerably from Houseman's; he found her meddlesome and "dictatorial." He resented her suggestions to Houseman and his co-director Jack Landau. On one occasion, seeing her whispering in Landau's ear, he called out, "Katie, don't do that. If there's something you want to say to me, come up and say it directly." Drake commented later, "She didn't much like that from me."

Drake was also upset with her puritanism, her obsession with cleanliness, and her new-found aversion to smoking (Drake smoked). Once, during an argument, Kate accused Drake of being used to leading ladies, not co-stars. Drake replied, "Well, at least they've been ladies."

"There's nothing you can say to me," Kate shot back, "that Spencer hasn't said to me much more!"

Despite their disagreements, Hepburn and Drake parted as friends. The two productions were financially successful, and Kate took them on tour with the intention of bringing them to Broadway. During the tour, however, she developed pneumonia, and frequently performed with a high temperature. To widespread disappointment, she decided not to take the shows to New York.

Kate with a more typical response to cameras as she walks along the island of Ischia on the Bay of Naples. There were rumors that she was planning to buy a house on the island, but she did not.

Robert Helpmann greets his old friend as Hepburn arrives in London for the filming of Tennessee Williams's *Suddenly, Last Summer*, May 25, 1959.

OPPOSITE Hepburn as Violet Venable, the malevolent matriarch of *Suddenly, Last Summer*. The story concerns Mrs. Venable's attempts to have her beautiful young niece lobotomized in order to cover up the terrible details of her son Sebastian's death. A sympathetic doctor gives the girl a truth serum instead, and she reveals in front of the entire family that Sebastian was a homosexual who used first his mother, then her, to lure young boys. His death was at the savage, cannibalistic hands of a roving band of street urchins in Italy.

ABOVE On the set, Kate prepares for a scene. The filming of *Suddenly, Last Summer* developed into the most distasteful movie experience of Hepburn's life. It is difficult to fathom why she accepted the part, because as filming progressed she began to hate her character, hate the play, hate all that the people in the scenario stood for. At one point she cried out to director Joseph Mankiewicz, "If you only knew what it means to me when I have to say those things!" All Mankiewicz could say in reply was, "That's the play, and that's what we have to do."

With the *Suddenly, Last Summer* set rife with rumors of discord and feuding, Kate, her co-stars Montgomery Clift and Elizabeth Taylor and their director Joe Mankiewicz stage a mock brawl for the benefit of photographers.

Although the report of a feud between Hepburn and Taylor was unfounded, there *was* considerable trouble on the set. Kate was very unhappy with what she perceived as Mankiewicz's bad treatment of Clift; Mankiewicz maintains he was the essence of patience with a man who was frequently drunk, usually late, and sometimes completely distracted and infantile.

OPPOSITE Although Kate seems fairly serene as she waits for a new scene to be set up, she was very nearly beside herself by the time the production wound up. She hated the woman she was playing, she despaired over Montgomery Clift's degeneration, she fought with Mankiewicz over matters big and small.

Ill at ease with Mrs. Venable, Kate wanted to play her as insane from the outset. Mankiewicz, true to the script, wanted to show her progressing from imperious self-control to pathetic madness. Kate was so insistent that Mankiewicz agreed to film two versions of Mrs. Venable's entrance—never intending to use the one Hepburn preferred. "Kate very much wanted to direct herself in *Suddenly, Last Summer*," Mankiewicz has said. "This is a battle I don't think a director can ever afford to lose . . . I insisted on the performance being played my way."

Perhaps the final straw for Kate was when Mankiewicz and cameraman Jack Hildyard decided to photograph her as harshly and unflatteringly as possible in the film's final scenes, to show her illusions of youth being stripped away along with her delusions about her dead son. Kate was very unhappy about this, especially since she had to catch on to what they were doing (removing the diffusion lens which had softened her appearance on camera) rather than being told up front about it.

All the tensions Kate felt exploded on the final day of shooting into an extremely uncharacteristic act. She walked up to Mankiewicz and asked him, "Are you absolutely through with me? I have nothing more to do with you or with the film?" When Mankiewicz said yes, she spat in his face, in front of a shocked crew.

ABOVE Mrs. Venable attends to her flesh-eating plant, one of the many symbolic aspects of the film. *Suddenly, Last Summer* was a very controversial movie. Many people felt that it dealt with its subject in a totally mature way, and that it paved the way for the adult-themed films that dominated the sixties. Others thought that it sensationalized a sensitive topic and catered to prejudice and ignorance.

Tennessee Williams, in fact, disliked this movie version of his "morality play." He wrote, "Brilliantly

(continued on page 150)

149

constructed as the screen version was by Gore Vidal, it still made unfortunate concessions to the realism that Hollywood is too often afraid to discard. And so a short morality play, in a lyrical style, was turned into a sensationally successful film that the public thinks was a literal study of such things as cannibalism, madness and sexual deviation."

Whatever the film's shortcomings, it was and remains an acting revelation. Elizabeth Taylor has rarely been better, and Hepburn, despite her problems with the part, brings the evilness of Violet Venable to life with a touch of genius. Tennessee Williams was thrilled: "Kate is a playwright's dream actress. She makes dialogue sound better than it is by a matchless beauty and clarity of diction, and by a fineness of intelligence and sensibility that illuminates every shade of meaning in every line she speaks. She invests every scene, each 'bit,' with the intuition of an artist born into her art."

Suddenly, Last Summer was one of the major films of 1959, and Elizabeth and Katharine were both nominated for Oscars. Neither won; in all probability they canceled each other out.

Hepburn refused to see the picture, and by all reports she has never seen it.

After the debilitating experience of *Suddenly, Last Summer,* Kate returned from England and spent a year resting and caring for Spencer. Not until the summer of 1960 did she decide to return to work, and she rejoined the Shakespeare Festival rather than make another film.

In June of 1960, she appeared as Viola in *Twelfth Night.* The critics weren't too kind to the production, but Kate, as usual, inspired praise. Walter Kerr wrote, "Miss Hepburn has always been one of the most fetching creatures to have been bestowed upon our time, and fetching isn't the half of it as the lady takes a stubborn, or a petulant, or a slightly fearful stance in her white ducks, brass-buttoned jacket, and sleek black boater."

OPPOSITE As Cleopatra in *Antony and Cleopatra,* July 1960. With Robert Ryan as Antony, this production fared somewhat better than *Twelfth Night* with audiences and critics. *Saturday Review* noted, "The production . . . is sprinkled with intelligence and assorted glimpses of Katharine Hepburn as Cleopatra. In the early scenes Miss Hepburn is surprisingly and happily unevasive, a half-naked woman with a genuine capacity for enjoying the wanton, sporting pleasures of the bed."

Despite Hepburn's presence, though, the season was only moderately successful. It was nine years before Kate did another stage play, and she never did Shakespeare again.

As Mary Tyrone in Eugene O'Neill's *Long Day's Journey into Night*. At first, Kate was terrified of playing this woman, a morphine addict whose tragic decline is revealed during one harrowing day with her family. Producer Ely Landau felt she would be perfect for the part, and he spent days cajoling her. Finally, she burst into tears. "I don't know whether I can do it. It's so demanding. I want to do it. I'm fascinated—but I'm terrified. It's so great!"

Kate again accepted the challenge—and agreed to take a salary of $25,000 instead of her usual $250,000 because the production would be a low-budget one which would relinquish nothing to Hollywood and stick to the very letter of the Eugene O'Neill play.

Landau wanted Spencer to play Mary's husband, a defeated actor. He went to breakfast with the couple. "It was extraordinary to watch her with Spence," Landau told Charles Higham. "She was a totally different person. She turned really submissive—it's the only word I can use—and hardly opened her mouth, other than introducing us."

Spencer mocked Kate's penchant for doing things "for no money" and said he would consider playing the role only if he were paid $500,000. It was an impossible demand—and more than likely Tracy's way of making sure he wouldn't have to play a role that must have intimidated him as much as Mary Tyrone did Kate.

With Dean Stockwell, Ralph Richardson, and Jason Robards, Jr., as the Tyrone family. Hepburn found the demands of this role exhausting, but knew instinctively that she needed to convey exhaustion in portraying the character. Mary Tyrone was a woman who could not have been more unlike Katharine Hepburn. Mary allowed herself to be defeated by life, allowed the dark forces of nature to consume her—something Kate Hepburn would never have dreamed of doing. Director Sidney Lumet was awestruck by Kate's performance: "It was the culmination of a lifetime of self-exploration; she found depths of feeling in herself that surprised and even shocked her."

Hepburn would allow nothing to stand in the way of her performance. Lumet recalls that he invited her to watch herself in the dailies, and she declined. "If I go to rushes," she explained, "all I'm going to be able to look at is this"—she indicated the flesh under her chin—"and this"—she grabbed the flesh under her arms. "I can't have all that distraction. I need all my energy to play the part."

Hepburn's portrayal of Mary Tyrone is considered one of the two or three greatest of her life. It is the essence of acting—becoming someone who was completely unlike herself, someone she had to struggle even to understand. Arthur Knight observed in *Saturday Review,* "Katharine Hepburn caps her distinguished career in the role of the pitiful, dope-addicted mother, groping back to the past for dimly remembered moments of happiness. Her transformations are extraordinary as, in recollection, she suffuses her tense and aging face with a coquettish youthfulness or, in the larger pattern of the play, changes from a nervous, ailing, but loving mother into a half-demented harridan."

Hepburn received her ninth Academy Award nomination for this film.

Long Day's Journey into Night marked the end of an era for Katharine Hepburn. She had been a movie star for thirty years, she had come back from being called "box-office poison" to reach the peak of her profession, she had developed from a mannered performer into a great tragedienne.

There was little more for her to conquer profession-ally, and she was far more concerned with Spencer's health than with her own career. Her father died shortly after *Long Day's Journey* opened, on November 20, 1962. Katharine was glad that she had been able to be with him at the end, sorrowful that she had not been able to spend more time with him over the previous year.

It was at this time that Katharine Hepburn decided she would retire from films and "be there" for Spencer. Her resolve was hardened when, on the way to a picnic with Kate, Spencer suffered a heart attack. Kate first called the fire department, then the Kanins and Mrs. Tracy. Kate and Louise Tracy took turns sitting vigil by Spencer's hospital bed, and when he was released, Mrs. Tracy left him in Hepburn's care.

For the next four years, Katharine Hepburn and Spencer Tracy spent life together without the distraction of work, sharing each other's company and love. Kate cared for Spencer every day, making him as comfortable as possible. In September of 1965 Tracy was hospitalized once again, with an inflamed prostate gland requiring surgery. Again, Kate and Louise Tracy sat with him in alternating shifts.

Spencer's health improved, and in 1966 outside forces began to come together that would result in the memorable final screen teaming of Tracy and Hepburn.

Part Six

COMEBACK

1967–1974

OPPOSITE Tracy and Hepburn on the set of *Guess Who's Coming to Dinner*. Spencer left it up to Kate to decide whether they should accept producer-director Stanley Kramer's proposal that they return to the screen. Kate felt it would be good for them, especially Spencer, after four years of professional inactivity.

And the story line appealed to Kate's liberal sensibilities: they would play a well-to-do white couple whose daughter wants to marry a black man. Spencer, too, wanted to appear in this film which urged racial tolerance and understanding in the troubled 1960s.

The film was an enormous risk for all concerned. Spencer's health was precarious; in order to obtain studio financing both stars had to waive their salaries, and Kramer had to personally accept responsibility for studio financial losses if Spencer died during production. Making the movie would be a strain on Spencer; but when this caused Kate to waver, he insisted that he wanted to make this important film, probably the last of his career.

On the studio lot with her niece, Katharine Houghton. Kate rather gently suggested her when the subject of casting the daughter in the picture came up. Kramer tested young Katharine and was impressed. She got the role.

FOLLOWING PAGES Spencer Tracy died ten days after filming was completed, on June 10, 1967. When the film opened in December, it was the heartbreaking culmination of the love affair between Tracy and Hepburn. Leo Mishkin wrote in the New York *Morning Telegraph,* "Both of them are so splendid, both of them are so beautifully matched . . . that a lump rises in the throat on the realization that they will never appear together again." Of Tracy, the *New Yorker* critic noted, "he turned his role into a stunning compendium of the actor's art . . . *Guess Who's Coming to Dinner* is the ninth movie that he and Miss Hepburn made together, over a period of twenty-five years, and when, at its climax, he turns to her and tells her what an old man remembers having loved, it is, for us who are permitted to overhear him, an experience that transcends the theatrical."

OPPOSITE The death of Spencer Tracy was a terrible blow to Katharine. She stayed away from his funeral so that it would not turn into a three-ring press circus.

A very important part of Katharine's life had ended. But she was not going to allow her life to end as well. Knowing that Spencer would want her to "get on with it," she quickly accepted a new role, Eleanor of Aquitaine in *The Lion in Winter*. "I don't want to think at all for two years," she said at the time. "I'm going to work hard. When I can think again, I'll retire."

In Nice to film *The Madwoman of Chaillot* (she had already completed her part in *The Lion in Winter*), Kate is congratulated by her director Bryan Forbes as they hear the news that she has won the Academy Award as Best Actress for *Guess Who's Coming to Dinner*. It was her second Oscar, thirty-four years after her first, and came on her tenth nomination. Spencer had also been nominated, and when Kate first heard the news, she inquired, "Did Spencer win, too?" Told that he had not, she said, "Well, that's O.K. I'm sure mine is for the two of us."

It was generally agreed that Kate's was a sentimental Oscar—she had deserved it far more in previous years—but no one cared. Many felt that it was about time all those wonderful Hepburn performances were acknowledged.

Later, Kate said, "I can't say I believe in prizes. I was a whizz in the three-legged race. That is something you can win. Not that it isn't extremely nice to get it. This one moved me. I think it was to Spencer and me as a team. That's why it pleased me."

OPPOSITE In London's Haymarket Theatre, Hepburn rehearses her role as Eleanor of Aquitaine in Anthony Harvey's film *The Lion in Winter*.

She had been approached to do the film just a few weeks after Spencer's death, and it was a perfect vehicle to take her mind off her sorrow: literate, funny, expressing universal truths about human nature, it also featured a stunningly well-rounded portrait of Queen Eleanor. Playwright James Goldman described her as "a handsome woman of great temperament, authority and presence. She has been a queen of international importance for forty-six years and you know it. Finally, she is that most unusual thing: a genuinely feminine woman thoroughly capable of holding her own in a man's world."

With Peter O'Toole as King Henry II. O'Toole and Hepburn adored each other—and clashed with each other—much as Eleanor and her king did in this story of royal family intrigue. Kate was typically bossy— "Peter, stop towering over me." "Peter, come and sit down." "Peter, don't be silly."

O'Toole would mutter under his breath that she was a "droning old bag," and say publicly that "she is terrifying. It is sheer masochism working with her. She has been sent by some dark fate to nag and torment me." But he also admitted, "Meeting Kate was the great experience of my life . . . If it had been twenty-five years before, I would have broken Spencer Tracy's fingers to get her!"

Interviewed on the set, Hepburn gave a picture of conciliation, despite O'Toole's misgivings. "We are going to get on very well. He is Irish and makes me laugh. In any case I am on to him and he is on to me."

Anthony Harvey directs Hepburn. Harvey had directed just one film before *The Lion in Winter,* a short subject, but Peter O'Toole admired it and brought Kate to see it. She was impressed as well, and told O'Toole if he believed in Harvey's talent, she would accept him as director.

Harvey was an excellent choice; the film is directed almost flawlessly. He and Hepburn got along well, despite his inexperience. This scene, in which Eleanor sits before her mirror and laments her lost youth, did present a problem between them, however. Kate was self-conscious about her appearance (the headdress surrounding her face was designed to hide what she felt was a crepelike neck), and she wanted to perform the scene with her hair up.

Harvey argued that Eleanor was alone in her bedroom, retiring for the evening, and she would let down her hair—both literally and figuratively. Kate was insistent that she was not going to do it; Harvey held his ground.

Finally, Hepburn relented, and she admitted that Harvey was right: the scene, brilliantly and movingly performed, is given just the right touch by Eleanor's small act of undoing her hair.

OPPOSITE On the set, Hepburn camps it up with one of the extras.

On location in Dublin, Kate plays an impromptu game of stickball. The filming was rife with problems: the weather was often bad; co-star Anthony Hopkins broke several bones in a fall off a horse, closing down production for several days; director Anthony Harvey contracted hepatitis, again interrupting filming. During rehearsals, Kate caught her thumb in a door and suffered a severe cut which caused her great pain throughout the production.

The strain got to Hepburn on one particular day. She requested the makeup man, and was told that he was busy with O'Toole. Kate, infuriated as much by the fact that she needed the makeup man as by the fact that he wasn't around ("It embarrasses me that I am always expected to be gorgeous") stormed into O'Toole's dressing room, shouted "Why won't you let me have my makeup man?" and socked O'Toole on the jaw.

Halfway back to her dressing room, she realized the absurdity of her actions and went into gales of laughter. Later, O'Toole appeared on the set with his head swathed in bandages, walking feebly on a pair of crutches.

OPPOSITE Many observers consider Hepburn's Eleanor of Aquitaine her greatest performance. She was by turns strong and vulnerable, imperious and needing, loving and cold-bloodedly scheming. Hepburn was able to present this complex and conflict-ridden personality without a single false note. For many, it is not only Kate's best performance, but one of the finest ever given on the screen.

Upon its release in October 1968, *The Lion in Winter* became Kate's second most successful film (after *Guess Who's Coming to Dinner*), helped along by reviews like Judith Crist's in *New York* magazine: "Katharine Hepburn certainly crowns her career as Eleanor, triumphant in her creation of a complete and womanly queen, a vulture mother who sees her sons too clearly, an aging beauty who can look her image in the eye, a sophisticate whose shrewdness is matched only by her humor. A pity it is that Miss Hepburn won an Oscar for sentimental reasons for last year's *Guess Who's Coming to Dinner,* when this year it would be hers by right of performance! She is simply stunning."

Hepburn was Oscar-nominated for the eleventh time, but the prevailing wisdom was indeed as Crist had suggested: it was quite rare for an actress to win the award two years in a row, and no one had won more than two Best Actress Oscars. What's more, almost everyone expected Barbra Streisand to win for her remarkable screen debut in *Funny Girl*.

In a wholly satisfying quirk of fate, Hepburn and Streisand received *exactly* the same number of votes, and shared the award—the only tie for Best Actress in Oscar history.

OPPOSITE Hepburn as Aurelia, the Madwoman of Chaillot. Kate was intrigued by Jean Giraudoux's character, a wild Parisian eccentric who takes it upon herself to thwart the plan of a group of capitalists to turn Paris into an oil field. She enlists the help of her equally mad friends to stymie the oilmen.

"I think *The Madwoman of Chaillot* has more relevance today than it did twenty years ago," Kate said during the spring 1968 filming in Nice. "The world has gone cuckoo. We're still dominated by greed, and that's what Giraudoux was talking about. The Madwoman represents the possibilities of man—she represents hope."

ABOVE Kate shares a laugh on location with co-star Danny Kaye. *The Madwoman of Chaillot* boasted an all-star cast including Charles Boyer, Edith Evans, John Gavin, Paul Henreid, Oscar Homolka, Margaret Leighton, Richard Chamberlain, Yul Brynner, and Donald Pleasance.

Filming went relatively smoothly, with just a few clashes between Kate and director Bryan Forbes. Kate received a barrage of idolatrous publicity following her Oscar win for *Guess Who's Coming to Dinner* (one article called her "Katharine the Great"), but she artfully avoided the press most of the time—the film was sev-

eral weeks into production before Kate even acknowledged the existence of the unit publicity man, whose job it was to bring stars and press together.

Kate did grant interviews occasionally, and in one she commented, "This is 'Be Kind to Kate' year. They'll turn on me."

ABOVE Kate bicycles to the set from her rented villa, wearing her "Madwoman" hat. After *The Madwoman of Chaillot* was released in 1969 "they" did indeed turn on Kate. The film was badly received, by critics and public alike. *Variety* summed up the general view: "Slow-paced pic holds slim box-office potential except for ardent Katharine Hepburn worshippers, who will be disappointed . . . Story of struggle between good and evil becomes audience's struggle against tedium. Film doesn't come off. Miss Hepburn, for example, fails to capture the fantasy-spirit of the Countess. Her performance suffers because of indecision. Instead of the Madwoman of Chaillot, Miss Hepburn is merely an extroverted eccentric."

Kate had little time to brood over the failure of her latest film. She was already in rehearsal for what was easily her biggest career stretch—a Broadway musical!

October 13, 1969: Hepburn displays a little nervousness as she absently chews on her scarf during rehearsals for *Coco*. Kate was jittery about playing the legendary Parisian fashion designer Coco Chanel, unsure that she could sing well enough to carry a musical, wary after her past Broadway failures.

Her nervousness manifested itself in high manic energy, and all the traits she had displayed in the past—bossiness, temperament, needing to have a say in *everything*—asserted themselves. Hepburn drove director Michael Bennett to distraction. "Strictly speaking, Kate would not allow me to direct," Bennett told Charles Higham. "When I asked her to sit she would stand, and when I asked her to go right she would go left, and so on. The thing to do was to ask for just what I didn't want so she would go where I wanted her to go after all. When I told her to exit left, she'd exit right, and I wanted her to exit right all along!"

A scene from *Coco*. While she was preparing for her role, Hepburn went to Paris to meet Coco Chanel. "At first I was petrified at the whole idea of meeting Chanel," she said. "Here I was, supposed to be meeting this great figure of fashion—and look at me! I've worn the same coat for forty years!"

Hepburn was awestruck by Chanel, afraid to meet her, convinced she was a breed apart—all the emotions most people feel upon meeting Katharine Hepburn. When they met, Kate was taken by her style, wit, and charm. After leaving her apartment, Kate realized she had forgotten something and went back. Coco Chanel was lying on her couch, napping. "Now I *knew* I could play her," Kate said. "She was a human being!"

In Cleveland during the *Coco* tour, Katharine leads the cast in a tribute to Coco Chanel, who died the night before, on January 10, 1971.

FOLLOWING PAGES Hepburn as Coco Chanel. She met what was perhaps her greatest challenge with such verve that she took over this elaborate, expensive, larger-than-life Broadway musical and made it her own. Her Coco was a bitchy, bossy, overpowering woman who by the sheer force of her personality makes everyone in her path fall madly in love with her.

Hepburn dominated the theater as few before her had, and she made audiences forget that the libretto was weak, the songs largely unmemorable and her own singing ability limited at best. She talked most of her songs, but Hepburn talks better than most people sing, so no one cared.

Audiences gave this virtuoso performance a standing ovation night after night, and *Coco* was a major hit. Hepburn stayed on Broadway for seven and a half months, after which she took the show on tour. Walter Kerr wrote in the New York *Times*, "The show has become a showcase, a form of endearment, a gesture of assent, an open palm of respect. Miss Hepburn will never be old enough or tired enough to undergo one of those official evenings of tribute at which everyone gathers to summarize and reminisce. And so it's been arranged right now, with her doing all the work. If *Coco* is anything, it is Miss Hepburn's gala Benefit Performance, for our benefit."

Hepburn clowns around with a fake witch's nose on location. Although Hepburn's Hecuba is passionate, raging, vengeful, and moving, critical consensus was that the film was static and uninvolving and it was not a hit.

OPPOSITE As Hecuba in Michael Cacoyannis' film version of Euripides' *The Trojan Women*. Kate traveled to Atienza, Spain for the filming. She wanted to do Greek drama because "my time is running out, and one wants to have done everything."

Most critical praise was reserved for the performances of Hepburn, Vanessa Redgrave, Genevieve Bujold, and Irene Papas. *Hollywood Reporter* critic Craig Fisher wrote, "There are real fires in this movie, however, generated by four intense and occasionally searing performances. In the largest role, Katharine Hepburn may, I think, be basically miscast, just as she was in *The Madwoman of Chaillot*. Her grief is peculiarly haughty, and she seems incapable of portraying abjectedness. But her presence provides a firm core for the movie and she has some great moments, especially when she hisses 'Kill her!' at Menelaus, when the Greek king is deciding what to do with Helen."

October 2 and 3, 1973. Katharine Hepburn does her first television interview, a two-night, three-hour marathon conversation with Dick Cavett.

Hepburn was not at all sure she wanted to do it, and most of the people around her advised against it. "My brother told me not to appear on this show," she told Cavett. "He said, 'They'll find out that you're a bore. They think you're great, don't expose yourself.' "

Kate did agree to come to Cavett's studio for some tests, to see if she'd be comfortable. Cavett told his cameraman to have film ready, sensing that this might be his only chance. He was right. After criticizing the color of the rug ("I'm personally going to dye it to-morrow morning") and asking that the table in front of her chair be replaced with a sturdier one she could put her feet up on, she allowed Cavett—still in shirt-sleeves—to roll the film and begin the interview.

She was an absolute delight. Feisty, funny, philo-sophical, condescending to Cavett, she riveted viewers with her ideas and personality. "Her energy seemed to increase as time went by," Cavett says, "and was still on the upswing when we quit." The interview lasted three hours, and Hepburn talked about everything— her childhood, her parents, breaking into houses as a young girl, her frequent firings from early plays ("I wasn't very good."), her early career, her world view.

Hepburn clearly ran the interview, with Cavett little more than an awestruck observer. She kept ignoring his frequent trivial interruptions until, at one point, she looked at him and said, "You're interrupting the long story of my life. If you'd just shut up—you never lis-ten!"

She was able to deflate Cavett with a single line. Never maliciously—just enough to make everyone laugh and keep his ego in check. At one point he began telling the story of having acted in a Stratford Shake-speare play with Hepburn. She didn't remember him. They were never on together, he explained, and he had only one line. "What was the line?" Hepburn asked. "Oh, I knew you'd do that—'Gentlemen, my master Antonio is at his house and desires to speak with you both.' "

Kate looked at him. "And is *that* the way you said it?"

It was the funniest moment in the broadcast. Amid the laughter of the people in the studio, Cavett said, "I've never walked off on a guest." Hepburn replied, "That's all right—you just go, and I'll take over."

(continued)

With Paul Scofield in the American Film Theater production of Edward Albee's *A Delicate Balance*. Hepburn agreed to do the Cavett interview primarily to promote this film, one of several made as part of an experimental series of "difficult" plays to be brought to the public as part of a subscription film series.

Kate at first didn't want to do the play, about a troubled Connecticut family and the disturbing influence of two intruders who insinuate themselves into the household. Kate said to producer Ely Landau, "What's it about? I'm a simple, nice person. I like to make Christmas wreaths, sweep floors, cook meals. I don't *understand* all this complicated stuff. I'm like my sister, who is a farmer and says the worst problem she wants is carrying two pails of milk over a fence."

Still, Kate—as usual—accepted the challenge. She believed strongly in Landau's effort to bring so-called "arty" films to a wider audience.

On the set, Kate gives a "Yes, sir!" salute to director Tony Richardson, with whom she had her usual quota of disagreements.

A Delicate Balance was one of the least successful productions in the American Film Theater series. Albee's very talky play did not translate well to the screen, and although the acting was uniformly good, not even Kate was able to make the play as emotionally involving as it should have been. As little more than a filmed stage play, the movie was a critical and commercial failure.

Cavett asked her how she had been able to remain on such a firm foundation when so many others in Hollywood ended tragically. "You certainly can never be helped by liquor and you can never be helped by drugs," she replied. "I've got plenty of energy without it. Cold sober, I find myself absolutely fascinating!"

Cavett asked, "Are you sorry you never acted with Olivier?"

Hepburn replied, "Well, neither of us is dead yet!"

Later, Cavett asked about her reported penchant for sleeping anywhere—lying down on top of a desk, for instance. "Is there a secret?"

"I just think I'm an old bore and I just go to sleep," Hepburn replied. "I lie down and I go to sleep. I do what I'm supposed to do. I come on the program, I talk. I'm supposed to talk, I talk. I go to bed and I sleep. I have food, I eat it. I'm very uncomplicated."

179

Sunday, December 16, 1973, Hepburn makes her dramatic television debut in Tennessee Williams's *The Glass Menagerie*. For years producer David Susskind had wanted Kate to play the role of Amanda Wingfield, the simple, sad, fallen Southern belle trying desperately to keep her family together. She resisted, principally be-cause one of her acting idols, Laurette Taylor, had originated the role and was unforgettable in it. But finally, she relented, especially after Susskind agreed to hire Anthony Harvey as the director. Kate called Harvey and said, "Live dangerously—let's do it!"

PAGES 182–183 With Sam Waterston as her son. Kate was rather miscast in the role of Amanda, although she tried her best to give the part as much reality as possible. "It's a great play. It really shows what lack of money can do to the human race. My father having been a Virginian, I understood Amanda's background in the South. I worked with one or two Southern ladies whom I knew, to get the accent right."

Anthony Harvey says: "Working with Kate is like taking on Cassius Clay for fifteen rounds. Her energy is phenomenal. I'd get to the studio at seven and she'd been there since six, riding around the grounds on her bicycle. She'd brought it down strapped on to the top of the car. She has a wonderful wild and lunatic passion for everything she does. It is a tremendously infectious sort of thing and she creates a state of excitement."

The telecast of *The Glass Menagerie* was well reviewed and generated high Nielsen ratings.

Four months after undergoing a hip operation, Hepburn makes her first appearance on an Academy Awards show to present the Irving Thalberg Award to her friend, producer Lawrence Weingarten.

Dick Cavett had asked her why she had never attended the ceremonies, despite eleven nominations and three awards. "Too gutless," she replied. "I was afraid I wouldn't win. It must be that. It couldn't be anything else. Or that I have no dress."

Hepburn wore a pantsuit the night of April 2, and threw aside her cane before striding purposefully onstage. She received a standing ovation, then looked out at the audience and said, "I'm surprised no one has shouted out, 'It's about time!' " She paused and then added, "It has taken me forty years to be unselfish."

Part Seven

GRANDE DAME

1975–1984

PREVIOUS PAGES "Neither of us is dead yet." Katharine Hepburn and Laurence Olivier in the ABC-TV presentation of George Cukor's *Love Among the Ruins,* March 6, 1975. Kate plays a widowed Shakespearean actress being sued for breach of promise by a young suitor. Olivier plays her barrister, a man with whom she had had a brief affair forty years earlier. The court case rekindles their love affair.

Clowning with Olivier and Cukor on the set. Cukor's first television film, and shot in just twenty days, *Love Among the Ruins* was a triumph when it was televised. Olivier and Hepburn played their colorful parts with panache, and their love scenes were touchingly effective. *Time*'s critic called the film "the most impressive evidence that age has its blessings." The two stars and their director were awarded Emmies by the Academy of Television Arts and Sciences.

OPPOSITE As the *grande dame* Jessica Medlicott in *Love Among the Ruins,* Hepburn looked particularly beautiful, and she enjoyed working with Olivier, an old friend. (She had, in fact, been the maid of honor at his wedding to Vivien Leigh in the 1930s).

Olivier facetiously told *Newsweek,* "I've been dreading this all my life." But, says George Cukor, "They got on very well. They appreciated each other, and liked working with each other. And the parts had *range,* which they don't always have in television."

Eula Goodnight takes some refreshment atop a horse. Despite her hip surgery, Hepburn continued to do her own stunts, refusing doubles for horseback riding and the raft sequences. "I haven't waited all these years to do a cowboy picture with Wayne to give up a single moment of it now," she said. Her energy and spunk seemed to reinvigorate Wayne, who had lost a lung to cancer and was cutting back on his physical activities. "Christ, she wants to do everything," Wayne groused. "She can't ride worth a damn and I gotta keep reining my horse in so she can keep up. But I'd hate to think of what this goddamned picture would be without her."

OPPOSITE Two Hollywood legends, together at last: Hepburn and John Wayne team up for *Rooster Cogburn,* the sequel to Wayne's Oscar-winning 1969 film *True Grit.*

Kate had professed an eighteen-year desire to "star in a Western with Wayne," and she snapped up the opportunity when it was offered to her. "I decided to grab him before it was too late—for me or for him."

Something of an *"African Queen* Goes West," *Rooster Cogburn*'s story concerns the hard-drinking marshal who teams up with a pious spinster, Eula Goodnight, to avenge the murder of her clergyman father. They chase the outlaws through the rough terrain of the high desert; they even shoot the rapids. As *Time* put it, "If the plot does not sound stirringly original, it at least gave the two aging stars a good workout."

On the last day of filming, Wayne and Hepburn embrace. They were indeed a mutual-admiration society. In a loving tribute for *TV Guide,* Kate wrote of Wayne: "He is so tall a tree the sun must shine on him whatever the tangle in the jungle below . . . His shoulders are broad—very. His chest massive—very. When I leaned against him (which I did as often as possible, I must confess—I am reduced to such innocent pleasures), thrilling."

Wayne: "I have never worked with a woman who has the smell of drama that this woman has. She is so feminine—she's a man's woman. Imagine how she must have been at age 25 or 30 . . . how lucky a man would have been to have found her."

The pairing of Wayne and Hepburn received considerable press attention, and was acknowledged by most critics as the only reason to see *Rooster Cogburn.* Hepburn, Vincent Canby commented in the New York *Times,* "has been too long glum in her recent films. It's good to see her looking as if she's having a lark for a change . . . In *Rooster Cogburn* Miss Hepburn has a roaring good time—so convincingly that you come to accept the movie on its own terms. It's a cheerful, throwaway Western, featuring two stars of the grand tradition who respond to each other with verve that makes the years disappear."

Rooster Cogburn, released in October of 1975, was a financially successful picture.

Hepburn trudges to the theater for the Broadway opening of Enid Bagnold's play *A Matter of Gravity,* February 3, 1976.

Kate is captured again—in a somewhat more receptive mood—outside the theater. *A Matter of Gravity,* by the eighty-seven-year-old author of *National Velvet,* concerns Mrs. Basil, an eccentric dowager who detests all things modern. She stays in one room of her thirty-room mansion and rails against free thinking, the sexual revolution, and the breaking down of class distinctions.

In an effort to modernize her opinions, Mrs. Basil's grandson brings home four friends—a homosexual couple, an intellectual liberal, and a hip young girl—with hilarious and intriguing results.

With Daniel Tamm. The character of Mrs. Basil could well have been patterned after Kate herself. During the run of the play, Hepburn, in several interviews, lamented the state of films, society, and moral values. "What on earth has happened to us? Instead of putting an end to all this, they tolerate it. Who is satisfied with this country? *Who?* . . . Life is still made up of the same damn old things that it was made up of when I did *Little Women*. Life is still made up of the love of friend for friend, mother for child, self-sacrifice, honor, and decency. Those things still go on. They haven't ceased to exist at all. They're just not written about anymore. They're considered boring subjects."

Kate takes a bow after a performance. *A Matter of Gravity* was well reviewed; it enjoyed a healthy run on Broadway and an extended tour. Dan Sullivan wrote for the Los Angeles *Times:* "Expecting to see Katharine Hepburn in Enid Bagnold's *A Matter of Gravity*, what we get, happily, is Enid Bagnold's *A Matter of Gravity* with Katharine Hepburn. That's not to say that Miss Hepburn fails to command the spotlight for a single moment . . . Though the manner is softer and giddier, she's as imperially herself here as she was in *Coco*. It is good sense, good business, and, as far as this reviewer is concerned, good art. Whoever wrote Katharine Hepburn was a genius. And yet this time hers isn't the dominant spirit. That belongs to Miss Bagnold, in whose mind the play is set and in whose voice all the characters—male, female, hybrid—talk.''

Kate with her two young co-stars Kevin McKenzie and Dennis Dimster in *Olly Olly Oxen Free*. It is the story of an eccentric old junk dealer who meets two irrepressible youngsters and helps them repair their grandfather's hot air balloon, which then accidentally inflates and takes them aloft.

"That man doesn't look like me at all," Kate snapped when she saw a stuntman double who was about to stand in for her in a scene in which her character grabs on to a rope hanging from the rapidly escaping balloon. The sixty-eight-year-old Hepburn did the stunt herself, to the astonishment of her co-workers. Kate was charmed by the script when it was sent to her by the young director Richard Colla. "I'll do it if you can find the money," she told him. It took two years, but he did raise the necessary capital. Kate took no salary, because Colla did not have a distribution deal; his plan was to make the film, then seek distribution. Hepburn would then receive a percentage of the profit.

"Why am I doing this picture? Because I've always wanted to fly in a balloon," Kate said during filming. "Doesn't everybody? I've flown an airplane, even though I never had a license. A balloon is different. Such a gay beauty!"

ABOVE AND OPPOSITE The climactic scene from *Olly Olly Oxen Free*, in which the runaway balloon lands in the Hollywood Bowl during a performance of the "1812 Overture." After the filming, Kate made an impromptu speech to the Bowl audience: "This should prove to all of you that if you're silly enough you can do anything."

Olly Olly Oxen Free is a delightful family film, and Hepburn's performance is funny and touching. Colla, unfortunately, was never able to get a major distribution deal. The film was not released until 1981, and it failed to find an audience. It became available on videotape through Time-Life Video in 1979, but it is Hepburn's "lost movie": some Hepburn filmographies, in fact, fail even to list it.

April 30, 1978. Kate helps pay tribute to the seventy-eight-year-old George Cukor at a Lincoln Center Film Society gala in his honor. Hepburn made a surprise appearance to introduce Cukor at the end of the ceremonies.

The two close friends were in the midst of plans to make their tenth film together, a television version of *The Corn Is Green.* Laughingly, Cukor told the press: "She's a tenant on my property in Los Angeles. I have to employ her to get the rent."

In December 1978, Hepburn submitted to a "Sixty Minutes" interview by Morley Safer in order to publicize *The Corn Is Green.* In her Manhattan townhouse, Kate pooh-poohed the acting profession: "I don't think it's any great art. Look at Shirley Temple. She was three and she was great. She could laugh and cry and carry on."

Why has Katharine Hepburn survived—indeed thrived—when so many of her contemporaries succumbed to the pressures of stardom? "I've lived in this house since 1931," Hepburn said. "Continuity. I live in a neighborhood where I've been known since I was a kid. I don't think of myself as being an actress. It's how much are you worth? Can you mend the window? Can you wash the window? Can you clean the house? Can you cook—wash the dishes? I live a different kind of existence . . ."

Several months after the telecast of this interview, "Sixty Minutes" approached Hepburn about airing some of the outtakes on a second segment. "No way," Kate replied. "I'm sick and tired of hearing Katharine Hepburn's opinions."

As Miss Moffat in the CBS-TV presentation of *The Corn Is Green* on January 29, 1979. At first, Kate turned down George Cukor's request that she star in this remake of the Bette Davis film, but when she reread the script she was struck by its warmth and reaffirmation of human values. The story revolves around a schoolteacher in Wales who helps a young miner realize his dream of an education despite his personal problems.

For this period role, Kate had the outfit she is wearing here reproduced from a photograph of her mother taken at the turn of the century.

FOLLOWING PAGES Kate and George Cukor walk the Welsh countryside on location. Hepburn, as usual, explored the area avidly, even to the point of going down into a pitch-black mine wearing a gas mask.

Kate's friendship with Cukor did nothing to dampen her creative combativeness. They fought so frequently, in fact, that at one point Cukor cried out, "For goodness' sakes, Kate, we might as well be married." Another time, he observed, "Our relationship is give and take. I give. She takes."

But Cukor was, as always, deeply impressed with Hepburn as actress, as were the critics, who greeted *The Corn Is Green* enthusiastically. "She surprises me in every scene," Cukor said. "She has such freshness and spontaneity. She never goes for the obvious effect . . . she plays it with more understanding than she would have thirty years ago, more forthrightly and humorously."

The Corn Is Green was a success. It marked the last time Katharine Hepburn and George Cukor would work together. Cukor, one of Hollywood's greatest directors, died in 1983.

February 6, 1979, an unusually elegant Hepburn attends a performance of Stephen Sondheim's Broadway musical *Sweeney Todd*.

OPPOSITE A self portrait by Katharine Hepburn. Entitled "Lizzie" after her character in *The Rainmaker,* the pen-and-ink and watercolor work was printed on a greeting card and sold during 1979 for the benefit of Actors and Others for Animals. The original is owned by Hal Wallis, producer of *The Rainmaker*.

A talented artist, Hepburn has produced many lovely paintings and sketches over the years, particularly landscapes and still lifes.

Dorothy Loudon and Kate in a scene from *The West Side Waltz*. The show had its premiere in Los Angeles the previous January, and traveled across the country before opening in New York. Hepburn's reviews were far superior to the play's—most critics found this effort of Thompson's far less interesting than *On Golden Pond*. But for Hepburn it was a triumph. Walter Kerr in the New York *Times:* "Although *The West Side Waltz* began its cross-country journeyings approximately one year ago, I'm not sure that author Ernest Thompson realizes even now what multiple small miracles Katharine Hepburn is bestowing upon his play . . . One mysterious thing she has learned to do is breathe unchallengeable life into lifeless lines. She does it, or seems to do it, by giving the most serious consideration to every syllable she utters. There may have been a time when she coasted on mannerisms, turned her rhythms into a form of rapid transit. That time is long gone. She is intensely concentrated now . . ."

Playwright Ernest Thompson kisses Hepburn onstage after the New York opening of his *West Side Waltz,* November 18, 1981. Kate saw Thompson's Broadway play *On Golden Pond* and was very impressed; she agreed to star in the screen version. Later, when she received his latest script, she was intrigued by the story of a seventyish widow whose fierce independence of mind is contrasted with her steadily declining physical condition; by the end of the play she has gone from a cane to a wheelchair. Dorothy Loudon plays a neighbor whose awkward attentions and mannerisms are a foil to the strait-laced Hepburn character.

Barbara Walters visits Hepburn on *The West Side Waltz* set for a two-part interview telecast in July and August 1981.

"I was terrified about meeting you," Walters said. "I was terrified about meeting *you,*" Hepburn replied.

The interview consisted mostly of Hepburn's opinions about things like current movies: "We're selling pornography—no question about that. Hard-core pornography—people are hard up for a thrill. They get confused, so they like to watch people fornicate."

Hepburn talked about her physical regimen: "I swim all winter you know, because I enjoy punishing myself—building my character, such as it is . . . I swim in Long Island Sound all winter, no matter what the temperature."

Walters asked Kate if she could touch her toes. "Of course," Hepburn replied. "Show us," said Walters. And Kate got up and touched the ground with her palms without the slightest hesitation.

"I have not lived my life as a woman," said Hepburn at one point. "I have lived it as a man. I've done what I damn well wanted and I've made enough money to support myself."

Later, Walters commented on the interview. "She said things that affected me deeply at this stage of my life. Having an adolescent child and a hectic career, I always felt torn apart. But Katharine, being so positive in her opinions, somehow strengthens one . . . In most interviews I am touched by the person, but I am not changed. Katharine Hepburn changed me."

PREVIOUS PAGES "Well, it's about time," said Katharine Hepburn as she met Henry Fonda after nearly fifty years in show business. The two had come together to film *On Golden Pond,* Ernest Thompson's successful play about an aged couple facing the man's decline and imminent death.

The first day on the set, Hepburn gave Fonda a gift—Spencer Tracy's favorite hat, which Fonda wore in the first scene. "He was so deeply moved," director Mark Rydell recalls, "that he started to cry." There was something of the Tracy/Hepburn relationship in the film's marriage, and—in the strange way life has of imitating art—in the Fonda/Hepburn working relationship as well. Henry Fonda was in failing health, this would clearly be his last film, and Katharine Hepburn was there to lend him support.

"It was a magical summer for both of us," Fonda said. "We worked together as though we'd been doing it all our lives. Kate is unique—in her looks, in the way she plays, most of all in herself. I love Kate for playing with me in this film."

"Their affection was palpable," Mark Rydell recalls. "One could feel it in the filming day to day. They approached this material bravely. Here you have Henry Fonda and Katharine Hepburn, both people in their seventies, dealing with material that has to do with the final years of one's life, and how do you face death and how do you support one another . . . it was quite a resonant experience."

ABOVE LEFT Ethel Thayer takes the boat out. In this, Kate's forty-fifth film (including TV movies) she was making something of a comeback to theatrical motion pictures. She was the only female star of her generation still working in major films, a remarkable testament to her tenacity, determination, and popularity. In fact, *On Golden Pond* and its enormous popular success introduced Katharine Hepburn to an entirely new generation of moviegoers. As *Time* put it in a November 16, 1981 cover story, "Spunky Kate and Honest Hank! If people were allowed to vote on such matters, the pair would probably be grandparents to an entire nation . . ."

ABOVE With Jane Fonda, who purchased the rights to *On Golden Pond* as a "present" for her father and who played the Thayers' estranged daughter, Chelsea. "My dad isn't exactly Norman Thayer," said Jane, "but there's a lot of Dad in the part . . . Like Chelsea, I had to get over the desperate need I once had for his approval, and to conquer my fear of him. We've never been intimate. My dad simply is not an intimate person. But that doesn't mean there isn't love."

Making *On Golden Pond* together was a form of therapy for both Henry and Jane, and their differences over the years were forgotten. The filming also made Jane think of her mother, who committed suicide when Jane was a little girl. "I couldn't help fantasizing what would have happened if [Kate] and my dad had be-
(continued)

Norman and Ethel go loon-watching. *On Golden Pond* was an enormous hit. Its moving story touched a nerve in the American public, and people poured into theaters to see it. Many of the reviews complained that the script was overly sentimental and clichéd, but to most moviegoers the central issues with which *On Golden Pond* dealt—the problem of aging with dignity; the difficulty of parent/child relationships—were handled in such a way that many were able to see themselves on screen, and they allowed themselves to be deeply moved without embarrassment.

Henry Fonda's performance was a revelation, and not only because we are seeing an actor bare his soul on camera. He breathes such life into Norman Thayer that the character becomes an amalgam of everything we know and love about Henry Fonda, while never losing the individuality of the person written by Ernest

Thompson long before Hank Fonda was signed to play him.

And Ethel Thayer, too, is the quintessential Hepburn role; a woman, as she put it, "of deep common sense, who finds joy in life and in the beautiful things around her. She's an authentic human spirit."

On Golden Pond received six major Oscar nominations: Best Picture, Best Director, Best Actor, Best Actress, Best Supporting Actress, and Best Screenplay. There was never any question that Fonda would win his first Oscar, but few expected Katharine Hepburn to win her fourth, especially since there was strong competition from Meryl Streep in *The French Lieutenant's Woman*. But, incredibly, she did.

Hepburn, once again, failed to appear at the ceremonies. Jane Fonda accepted the award for her ailing father. Several weeks later, Henry Fonda died.

---

come lovers forty years ago, and Kate had been my mother.

"To work with her, and to work with my father, was a terrifying, waking up in the morning wanting to throw up kind of experience. But what happened was, when we went to rehearsals I realized that she was as nervous as I was!"

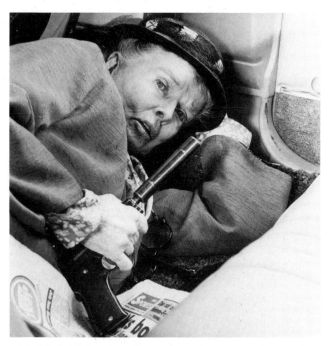

OPPOSITE Hepburn as Grace Quigley in her most recent film, *The Ultimate Solution of Grace Quigley,* released in the fall of 1984. Hepburn tried for more than ten years to get this project in front of the cameras, but when she did it wasn't at all certain she would be able to act in it. In the fall of 1982, while driving near her Connecticut home with her companion Phyllis Wilbourn, Hepburn lost control of her car and drove it into a tree, injuring both women seriously. It was reported that Hepburn had broken her ankle, but she had actually almost lost her foot, which was very nearly severed to the point of hanging by a tendon. Doctors reattached the foot and hoped that Hepburn's indomitable spirit would help speed the healing process. It did.

"They told me I was going to lose the foot, but I didn't," she said in the New York *Times,* "and I didn't have to give up my exercises, which I love. I'm so grateful. I'm lucky. I've kept myself in good trim, and here I am and I'm still working, and that's why I wanted to do this movie so much."

ABOVE Nick Nolte, as Seymour Flint, takes Grace for a spin on his motorcycle. *Grace Quigley,* directed by Anthony Harvey, is the blackest of black comedies, about an old woman who hires a hit man to end her unhappy life. Instead, they begin helping other desperate old people end their lives.

The script came to Hepburn in 1972, when it was thrown over her fence by its author, Martin Zweiback. By the time he got back home, Kate had left a message on his answering machine—she loved it. But no studio wanted to touch it, even with Hepburn as star. "Subject matter," says Zweiback. "Old age and death, these were not what they were looking for."

Finally, Cannon Films agreed to finance the venture,

with Nick Nolte signed as co-star. Upon meeting Nolte, Kate said, "I understand you've been in every gutter in town, sir." To which Nolte replied, "Yeah, Kate, I've hit 'em all." A friendship developed, based partly on Kate's determination to lead still another co-star along the straight and narrow. Nolte's assessment of Hepburn? "She's just a cranky old broad who's a lot of fun."

ABOVE RIGHT Grace hides in the back of a Cadillac as she prepares to complete another hit job. Hepburn feels this film's message is an important one. "When the body goes, or the mind goes, and it's time to say goodbye, why shouldn't you? Will they take away your right to choose? Death does not horrify me. I've been the luckiest of human beings. I'm grateful for that. If I had lost that foot, I wouldn't roar and groan. As long as I have places I love to go, or a wonderful job . . . The two things that keep you going are love and work—being occupied."

That Katharine Hepburn, after fifty years in Hollywood, is still starring in top-notch films is a testament to her astonishing zest for life. After chronicling such a long career, an author might be forgiven for summing it up as though its end were close at hand. But with Hepburn, to write *finis* is to take the risk of later appearing the fool. Who knows how many more films may star Katharine Hepburn? How many more awards she may add to her crowded mantelpiece?

The extraordinary life she has led may well hold untold future enrichments for all whom she touches with her spirit, strength, warmth, and wit. And if love is "one of the things that keep you going," the public's affection for Kate Hepburn should make her unstoppable for a long time to come.

About the Author

James Spada is the author of the bestselling *Streisand: The Woman and the Legend, Monroe: Her Life in Pictures,* and *Judy and Liza,* as well as three other books. His books have been serialized in *People, McCall's,* the *Ladies' Home Journal, Cosmopolitan,* the London Sunday *Times* Magazine, the New York *Daily News,* the New York *Post,* the Philadelphia *Inquirer,* the London *Daily Mirror,* the Chicago *Tribune* and by the New York *Times* Syndicate.

His interview subjects include Gore Vidal, James Michener, Stephen King, Robert Redford, Barry Gibb, Julie Harris, Norton Simon, Studs Terkel, Mike Nichols, Sydney Pollack, and Jan-Michael Vincent.

Born and raised in Staten Island, New York, Mr. Spada now lives in Los Angeles, where he is at work on his next book, *Meryl Streep*.

Photo Sources

Academy of Motion Picture Arts and Sciences Library
Joseph Abeles
Bennett's Archive
Bettmann Archive
Ben Carbonetto Collection
Bill Chapman
Homer Dickens Collection
Museum of Modern Art Film Stills Archive
Sandra Quinn Collection
United Press International